# HISTORIC HOUSES IN FUJIAN

///////////////////////

• EARTHEN FORTRESS

QU LIMING / CHEN WENBO

福建经典古民居

土堡

摄影\曲利明

撰文\陈文波

海峡出版发行集团

海峡书局

# 乱世风华　福建"堡"藏

2008年7月7日，从加拿大魁北克城召开的世界遗产大会上，传来一个令人振奋的消息："福建土楼"被正式列入世界文化遗产名录！深藏大山中的福建土楼"一举成名天下知"。

随后的事情，大家都知道了：福建土楼进入了"黄金时代"，走上了保护和发展的"快车道"。福建土楼，环境越来越好；福建土楼，人气越来越旺；福建土楼，名气也越来越大。

同样是在福建，同样藏在大山深处，同样是大型的夯土建筑，"福建土堡"这样独特的建筑形式似乎没有赶上好日子。直到第三次全国文物大普查，这样奇特的建筑形式才渐渐为人所知，并得到学者专家们广泛认同和赞叹：

"土堡是继土楼之后的又一重大发现，都属于珍贵的文化遗产。"

——这是已故的古建筑权威罗哲文先生的判断。

"土堡和福建土楼一样，都是中华民族传统民居建筑文化中极珍贵的一笔文化遗产……在中国古代建筑史中占有其他民居无法取代的重要地位。"

——这是来自清华大学建筑学院王其钧教授的高度评价。

"土堡这种以防御为主、居住为辅……的民居建筑形式，值得我们去认识、研究、保护和发扬光大。"

——这是厦门大学建筑系教授戴志坚的呼吁。

"这些土堡具有制定世界文化遗产的分量，是全人类的文化资产，当然值得保存和保护，子子孙孙永宝用，而且，是整合性保存，也就是活的保存。"

——这是台湾大学夏铸九教授的建议。

……

那么，土堡是什么？它从哪里来？它和土楼又有什么样的关系？

我们先翻开字典，在《辞海》中，土堡是指"土筑的小城"；在《现代汉语词典》里，对于堡字，有三种注释，最贴切的应该就是"当读音为bǎo的时候，其意思为'土筑的小城，为军事用途，例城堡'"。

显然，土堡，从这个词语诞生之日起，就注定要与乱世干戈纠结一生。正如《三国演义》的开篇所说的一样，"天下大势，分久必合，合久必分。"战乱，似乎贯穿着中华文明的历史。从三国两晋时代的坞堡，到今天的土堡，那夯筑土墙的声音里，是不是有着某种关联呢？

让我们走进历史深处，寻找问题的答案。

福建最早关于土堡的记载，来自清朝同治年间出版的《宁化县志·建邑志》中的一段文字"……隋大业之季，其时土寇蜂举，黄连人巫罗俊者，年少负殊勇，就峒筑堡卫众，寇不敢犯，远近争附之……"

隋末唐初，天下大乱之际，在社会失去正常秩序的时候，人们必须寻找一种保护自己的方法。少年英雄巫罗俊的办法就是筑起土堡，用结实的堡墙围住乡亲，也围住了安全。当然，土堡就是在乱世中不得已出现的产物。历史典籍中，虽然找不到土堡与坞堡的渊源，但人类趋利避害的本能，注定了土堡出现的必然。

中国古建筑的权威罗哲文先生是这样定义土堡的出现："土堡是在特殊的历史时期、特殊的地理环境、特殊的社会形态中产生出特别的防御性乡土建筑。"

特殊的历史时期——那就是乱世。人在不安定的环境下，会本能地要寻找一种安全感。隋唐兵燹，宋元更替，明清战乱，改朝换代的时候，就是土堡流行的时候。所以专家们考证：土堡始于隋唐，成熟于宋元，盛行于明清。

特殊的地理环境——山地丘陵间，天高皇帝远，地下有资源，山中有匪寇。福建有土堡的地方，基本上都在山区，在这样的地方，即使是所谓的太平盛世，也有阳光照不到的地方。为了安全，人们只能筑起高高的土堡，躲进小楼成一统。

特殊的社会形态——宗族的力量。当政府都自顾不暇，秩序无从保障的时候，只有同宗同族的号召力，促使乡民们抱团取暖。今天在八闽大地上留存的土堡，大的几千平方米，小的也有几百平方米，无一不是规模浩大的工程，如果不倾全族之力，是很难筑就的。

特别的防御性乡土建筑——土堡，从诞生起，每一个设计，每一个元素的目的都是为了防御。为了安全，建筑的形状、外观，都是次要。

所以，今天，我们才能在八闽大地上看到那么多形态各异，丰富多彩的土堡建筑。这些土堡充分利用自然环境，因地制宜，构筑巧妙奇特——他们或在山冈上，或在水田间，或在山坡下，或在民居中，鹤立鸡群，绝世独立，绽放出绝美的容颜。

走进土堡，你很难不被我们先人的智慧所折服，构成土堡的每个元素都别具匠心，为了守护自己的家园，筑造者们在土堡的DNA链条上，深深地印烙上"防御"两个字。

因为这是乱世，因为这是一个随时都有可能失去财产、尊严、甚至生命的时代。我们的祖辈，那些大多数都是与大地打交道的人，即使活得卑微，依然日出而作，日入而息，用汗水浇灌土地，期待每一分微薄的收成，只为了活下去。

这是一种何等坚强的信念，为了家园，为了家人，他们筑造起高高的堡墙，守卫着。

走近土堡，最具视觉冲击力的，当属厚实的堡墙。这是土堡的第一道屏障，与土楼、围屋不同，土堡的堡墙往往是单独夯筑的围墙，并不作为承重墙使用。而且，堡墙的基础往往是深埋高砌的石墙，毛石之间的缝隙再用三合土勾抹。用"质量就是生命"形容土堡的筑造，并不过分，高大石墙以上部分的夯土，则是根据地质环境的不同，配比而成。为了更加牢固，一些土堡在夯墙的时候，还会掺入石灰、红糖、糯米浆等等，真正地达到坚不可摧。为了保持堡墙的韧性，我们的先人，还会在夯筑堡墙时，加入毛竹和杉木板一起夯打，增强堡墙的拉力。这样筑造的堡墙，能耐火烧，经得起枪击炮打，而"岿然不动"。

一味地挨打也不是办法，土堡自然有反击之道。

在厚重的堡墙后，往往是一圈贯通全堡的跑马道。所谓跑马道，就是用土夯筑，在堡墙内圈的防御通道。道能跑马，意味着宽敞畅通。福建土堡无论大小，基本都筑有跑马道，有了跑马道，土堡就有了防守反击的阵地。有了跑马道，当时土堡堡墙夯筑时的一些细节设计就派上了用场。

细心的参观者在走进土堡时，往往会发现，土堡的墙上布满了大大小小的洞。这就是竹制枪孔，遍布整个堡墙，实现火力的全交叉，让打击无死角。竹制枪孔的发明和运用，直接让土堡从乌龟变成刺猬，匪徒来犯，无从下口。

除了竹制枪孔，斗式的条窗，既保证了采光，又能在防御的时候派上用场。在门洞的防守上，筑造者除了给沉重的木质大门包上铁皮外壳外，门洞上方的注水孔和注水槽，直接扑灭了敌人妄图用火攻堡门的企图。

单靠堡墙还不够，福建土堡在防御功能上发挥到了极致，可攻可守的碉式角楼，扩大了视野，占领了制高点，成为整个土堡防守的中心。

这样一整套的防守设计，加上筑造土堡都会挖上一口水井，只要粮食储备足够，即使敌军围困万千重，土堡内的生活秩序依然有序。一些土堡甚至备有鸽子笼，意味着关键时刻还能放出信鸽，对外求援。

这样的土堡，谁能攻下？

跟时间赛跑，谁都是输家。

即使是再坚固的堡垒，都敌不过岁月的侵蚀，熬不过光阴的流逝，曾经的高大壮观，变成残垣断壁，曾经的人声鼎沸，依然人去楼空。

根据不完全统计，历史上，福建土堡的数量曾经上万，如今，登记在册，有名有姓的土堡不过几百座，土堡基本形制还在，堡内建筑还在的土堡不会超过一百座，而尚在"原生态"，保有"原真性"的土堡，不过几十座而已。

这些土堡分布在福建三明的大田、尤溪、永安、沙县、将乐、宁化、清流、明溪、梅列、三元；泉州的德化、永春、安溪、南安；福州的永泰、闽清、福清、闽侯；龙岩的漳平；宁德的古田等地。

这不是危言耸听，就在我们寻找土堡、记录土堡的同时，土堡也在一步步走向消亡，你翻看本书时，图片上尚保存完好，也许，它早已消失了。

土堡的保护，也需要与时间赛跑。

安贞堡是最早被列入国家级文物保护单位的土堡，当时，福建土堡这个概念尚未提出。福建土堡的再认识，始于第三次全国文物普查，这项工作2007年4月开始，2011年12月结束，历时五年。五年里，福建土堡被再次认识，终于引起了社会的关注。

2013年，由安良堡、芳联堡、光裕堡、广崇堡、琵琶堡、绍恢堡、泰安堡等七座土堡打包组成大田土堡群，被列入第七批全国重点文物保护单位。

一大批土堡也走在成为全国文物保护单位的路上。

福清的东关寨；永泰的青石寨；尤溪的聚奎堡、茂荆堡、书京土堡；沙县的水美土堡；永安的复兴堡、福临堡；将乐的勘厚堡；永春的巽来庄；安溪的西坪土楼；漳平的泰安堡……都已经被列入省级重点文物保护单位。

他们在与时间争分夺秒，为了守护人类的珍贵遗产。

房子是需要人气的。

游客们在走进土堡，但土堡里的人正在搬离土堡。这不是围城，这是现实。

从土堡出来，我们回到现实。如今，堡里的人正在远离土堡。我们在寻找记录土堡的同时，我们遗憾地发现，如果不是没有办法，没人愿意住在土堡里。

走出土堡的土堡人，在曾经的祖宅边上盖起了火柴盒的楼房，通上电，用上自来水，儿时的房子，偌大的土堡，正好用来堆放杂物，或者养鸡。而盖在山冈上的堡寨，因为交通不便，早已被荒草掩埋。

鸡、猪，当然还有虫、蛇等生物，渐渐地成了土堡的主人。

曾经的祖宅，曾经的记忆，渐行渐远，远走的人，可能依稀会记得凤阳堡、会清堡、东关寨等名字，那是他们遥远的乡愁，回不去的故乡。

我们必须承认，土堡，这一建筑模式正在走向消亡，我们试图挽留，但就像指间流逝的沙，却无可奈何，无能为力。

没有了居民，土堡就没了生气，没有人间烟火的熏润，土堡的活性保护就无从谈起。

最后，留下的，只能是一声叹息。

# Elegance in Tumultuous Times
## -A Trip to Fujian Earthen Fortress

On Jul. 7, 2008, an exciting tiding arrived in the World Heritage Convention held in Quebec, Canada: "Fujian Tulou" was officially enrolled in the Directory of World Cultural Heritage! Though tucked away among the mountains, "Fujian Tulou" achieved world fame instantly.

Then, it occurred a series of events that are already known to all: Fujian Tulou entered "an golden age" and the "expressway" featured by protection and development. Its environment becomes much and much better, with its number of tourists on the increase, thus gaining fame in more and more regions.

However, it seemed that "Fujian Tubao", another special architectural structure and large building made by rammed earth in the depth of the mountains of Fujian never saw its good days. Actually, it was gradually known by people after the 3rd National Census of Cultural Relic. Since then, it received a wide recognition and acclaim among scholars and experts –

"Tubao is another important discovery after Tulou, and they are both valuable cultural heritages."

This is the judgment of the deceased Mr. Luo Zhewen, the authority in the ancient architecture.

"Like Fujian Tulou, Tubao is a priceless cultural heritage in the architectural culture embodied by the traditional civil dwelling of Chinese people ... it has a significant position which cannot be replaced by other civil dwellings in the ancient Chinese architectural history."

This is the high praise given by Prof. Wang Qijun from School of Architecture of Tsinghua University.

"Such a kind of civil dwelling with the main purpose of defense while also considering residential function ... deserves of learning, research, protection and promotion."

This is the appeal of Prof. Dai Zhijian of Department of Architecture of Xiamen University.

"These Tubaos has a significance for which it can be established as world cultural heritage. They are the cultural properties of all human-beings, and thus is worthy of protection and conservation. We and our offspring should treasure it and preserve it as a whole structure – that is to keep its vitality. "

This is the suggestion of Prof. Xia Zhujiu from Taiwan University.

Well, what is Tubao? Where does it come from? What kind of relationship does it bear with Tulou?

Let us first consult the dictionary. According to "Ci Hai", bao means "a small town made by earth"; in "Modern Chinese Dictionary", there are three explanations of bao, the most appropriate one being "when the pronunciation is bao, it means 'a small town made by earth, for military purpose, such as castle'".

It seems without saying that the world Tubao was destined to be involved with wars and tumultuous times after it was created. Just as it goes in the first chapter of "Romance of Three Kingdoms", "The world under heaven, after a long period of division, tends to unite; after a long period of union, tends to divide." Turbulent times and division seem to run through the history of Chinese civilization. From Wubao in Western Jin and Eastern Jin's

Periods to Tubao as we call nowadays, a sound comes from the same rammed earth, which makes us reflect on it: do the two structures have a kind of relationship?

Let us make an in-depth study of history to find the answer to the question.

According to the earliest records about Tubao in Fujian, there is a paragraph in "Record of Jianyi, Ninghua County Annals" published during the rein of Tongzhi in Qing Dynasty which writes that "... During the warring days of Sui Dynasty when bandits were rampant, Wu Luojun from Huanglian, a young man with all courageousness, built the Tubao near the cave to defend against the enemies for people; therefore, bandits dared not intrude it and people far and near came to seek shelter from him..."

At the end of the Sui Dynasty and the beginning of the Tang Dynasty, the world was in a state of chaos while the society was in disorder, which compelled people to find their own ways of protection. The young hero Wu Luojun built his Tubao to protect his townsfolk and surrounded them with solid walls which also guaranteed security. Obviously, people were forced to build Tubao in such a period. In the ancient historical books and records, though we could not find the relation between Tubao and Wubao, it was the people's instinct of playing up strength and avoiding weakness that made it a necessity to create Tubao.

Mr. Luo Zhewen has made such a definition about Tubao: "Tubao was created as a special defensive building with local features in a particular historical period, a particular geographical environment and a particular social mode."

Particular historical period – it means tumultuous time. Under an insecure environment, people will seek a sense of security by the light of nature. Tubao prevailed when the old dynasty was replaced by a new one, such as the riotous and transitional period between Sui Dynasty and Tang Dynasty, Song Dynasty and Yuan Dynasty, and Ming Dynasty and Qing Dynasty. As a result, experts after textual research found that: Tubao was created in Sui and Tang Dynasties, improved in Song and Yuan Dynasties and gained popularity in Ming and Qing Dynasties;

A particular geographical environment – hemmed by mountains and hills, far away from the rein of the royal court, the region was abundant in resources underground with bandits harassing and wrecking. Those places in Fujian where Tubao was built mostly reposed in mountainous regions. For such a region, even in flourishing age, sunshine could not shed its light into it. For safety, people were forced to build high-rise Tubao and hide themselves behind it, creating their own world;

A particular social mode – the power of the clan. When the government could hardly protect itself, when the social order could not be guaranteed, only the appeal of the clan could make people gather together for defense. Tubao is a large-scale project, which could not be accomplished without the efforts of the entire clan;

A special defensive building with local features – Tubao was from the day of creation immersed with defense and safety, bodied forth by each design and each element; therefore, the shape and appearance do not matter at all.

Hence, today, we can see so many Tubaos with great diversity and variety across Fujian. These Tubaos made a telling use of the natural environment, adjusting the design to local conditions and boasting of ingenuity and peculiarity – some of them are situated in the hillock, some in the paddy field, some at the foot of a hill, and some among other civil dwellings, but they excel other architectures with their peculiarity, like a unique flower in full bloom.

Entering Tubao, you can not help admiring the wisdom of our ancestors. Every element made up of Tubao is original. In order to guard against their home, the builders inscribed the word defense deep into the DNA duplex of the fortress.

This is a tumultuous time, where they can lose wealth, dignity and even life at any time. Our forefathers are mostly those farming the land. Even though they lived a humble life, they began to work early and finished it late. Their sweats watered the land and in their heart, each grain of rice was expected to be reaped so that they can survive.

What kind of persistence this is. For homeland and family, they built towering walls to keep guard.

Coming close to Tubao, you will find the most striking image is the thick and solid walls. This is the first defense. Different from Tulou and Hakka Walled House, the wall of Tubao is often built by rammed earth as the bounding one instead of the main one. Besides, the foundation of the wall was laid deeply into the earth and the height of it is soaring. The gaps between the rubbles are plastered by trinity mixture fill. For the construction of Tubao that values quality as life, it is reasonable. The rammed earth above the tall wall is mixed in different proportions according to different geographical environments. For solidarity, lime, brown sugar and sticky rice plasm would be used to make it undefeatable in real sense. For tenacity, our ancestor will add in bamboos and Chinese fir boards to increase the tensile force of Tubao. Such a type of Tubao is fire-resistant, guards against bullets and bombs and "stands unshakable".

But it certainly can not work if it just defends; Tubao has its own way of fighting back.

Behind the thick walls, there is often a circle of racing course running around the entire building. The so-called racing course is a defense pathway made by rammed earth within the inner part of Tubao. As horses can run on it, it is wide and smooth. Whatever size a Tubao has, it basically has its racing course so that people can find a way to defend and fight.

With the racing course, some detailed designs are useful.

Inside Tubao, some circumspective people will find that the walls of Tubao are filled with a variety of holes in different sizes. These are the bamboo-made gun holes; during the battle, they can cover the entire wall with machinegun fire so that no dead angle is left. The invention and application of bamboo-made gun holes can turn Tubao from a turtle into a hedgehog. If bandits wanted to invade Tubao, they would find it hard to initiate an attack.

Besides bamboo-made gun holes, the strip-pattern window in bucket type can guarantee lighting and defense. For the gate, the builder enclosed the heavy and wooden gate with a piece of steel sheet. The water injection hole and water injection channel in the upper side of the gate made it impossible for enemies to launch a fire attack to the gate.

With the walls, it is just not enough. In defense, Fujian Tubao is consummate. The fort-type turret enlarges the view and takes up the commanding height, becoming the center of defense.

Such a complete set of designs for defense, with a well usually dug out during construction and enough food, people can maintain the living order in Tubao even there are thousands of enemies besieging it. Some Tubaos even have pigeon house, which means that in significant moments, carrier pigeons can be released to ask for help.

For such a kind of Tubao, who can conquer it?

He who runs with time is a loser.

Whatever strong the fortress is, it can not stand erect with the erosion of the time. With the sands of the time running by, the once high-reaching and imposing Tubao became ruins and dilapidated walls; the hustle and bustle of Tubao disappeared into thin air.

According to incomplete statistics, there had been over ten thousand Tubaos in Fujian. Nowadays, the number of those registered in the book with their own names can not exceed several hundred. The number of those with the basic structure and the inner part preserved can not exceed one hundred. The number of those with "original ecology" conserved and "originality" kept can not exceed a few.

These Tubaos are scatted in some cities of Fujian Province, such as Sanming City: Datian, Youxi, Yong'an, Shaxian, Jiangle, Ninghua, Qingliu, Mingxi, Meilie and Sanyuan; Quanzhou City: Dehua, Yongchun, Anxi and Nanan; Fuzhou City: Yongtai, Minqing, Fuqing and Minhou; Longyan City: Zhangping; Ningde: Gutian.

This is not an alarmism. When we are looking for and recording Tubao, it comes to extinction gradually. When you turn over a page of this picture album and see the well-preserved Tubao, you may not imagine it has already vanished.

The protection of Tubao should compete with time.

Anzhenbao is the first Tubao to be listed as State Protected Historic Site. Then, the concept of Fujian Tubao was not raised. The second time people learned about Fujian Tubao was in the 3rd National Census for Cultural Relic, which lasted 5 years from Apr. 2007 to Dec. 2011. In those 5 years, Fujian Tubao was learned by the society again and eventually seized the attention of all.

In 2013, Datian Tubao Cluster, made up of Anliangbao, Fanglianbao, Guangyubao, Guangcongbao, Pipabao, Shaohuibao and Taianbao, was enlisted in the 7th batch of the National Key Cultural Relics Protection Units.

A large number of Tubaos are on the way to be listed as State Protected Historic Site--

Those already listed as the Provincial Key Cultural Relics Protection Units include Dongguanzhai in Fuqing, Qingshizhai in Yongtai, Jukuizhai, Maojingbao and Shujing Tubao in Youxi, Shuimei Tubao in Shaxian, Fuxingbao and Fulinbao in Yong'an, Kanhoubao in Jiangle, Xunlaizhuang in Yongchun, Xiping Tulou in Anxi and Taianbao in Zhangping.

They are racing against time and catching every minute in saving this valuable heritage for human-beings.

A house needs popularity.

When tourists walk into Tubao, the people living within are moving out of it.

This is not Fortress Besieged, this is reality.

Coming out of Tubao, we return to the reality. The residents of Tubao are getting away from it. When recording Tubao, we found it a regret to notice that no one is willing to live inside if there is a way out.

Those former residents built matchbox-like houses beside their ancestral home. With electricity and running water, they enjoy the benefits of modernization while the house they once lived in their childhood, the large Tubao is used to store sundries and raise chicken. For Tubao built in the hillock, it has been covered by verdure and forgotten by people due to traffic inconvenience.

Chicken, ducks, pigs, and of course birds, rats, bugs, snakes and other creatures became masters of Tubao.

The former ancestral home and the past memory are fading away. The people left might remember the names of Tubao, those XXbao, XXlou, XXzhai and etc. Those are their nostalgia from far away, and their hometown that they cannot return.

We must admit that Tubao, such a kind of construction mode is vanishing. We try to prevent it, but like the sands slipping through fingers, they are unavoidable and inevitable.

Without residents, Tubao has no popularity. Without the common people in the earthly world, Tubao is dead. The so-called vitality protection is out of question.

Finally, what is left, is just another sigh.

# 目录/CONTENTS

# 福建土堡分布示意图/Distribution map of Fujian earthen fortresses

沙县

三明市

清流县

尤溪县

闽清县

福州市

永安市

永泰县

福清市

大田县

德化县

永春县

漳平市

龙岩市

泉州市

漳州市

漳浦县

福建土堡被发现，被研究，成为学界和世人所瞩目的建筑，源于三明土堡群的被发现和被认知。目前，福建土堡数量最集中、种类最繁复的土堡基本上都在三明。

三明各地均有土堡，但现存完好的土堡仅50余座，主要集中在大田、尤溪、永安、沙县等地。

大田土堡相对集中，种类杂，形制多，土堡文化丰富。目前被列入第七批国家级文物保护单位的七座土堡均位于大田，其特色性、系统性和建筑的精美性都具有相当高的水准。沙县土堡侧重砖土木结构，生活设施齐全，比较集中，其代表性土堡就是水美土堡群。尤溪土堡的特点为大型土堡多，高台阶、多台基的土堡多，由土堡衍生出的堡屋、堡楼、堡居等防御性建筑多，尤溪土堡建筑复杂，装饰艺术华丽，精美土堡层出不穷。永安土堡建筑精巧，从外观建筑结构到内部的装饰工艺都独具匠心。

三明其他县市如清流、将乐、宁化、三元等地也有土堡存在，不过数量较少，保存完好的不多。将乐的勘厚堡、三元的松庆堡为少有的精品。

The discovery and recognition of Sanming Earthen Fortresses is the first chapter of the exploration and research of Fujian earthen fortress, which now stands as an eye-catching architecture in the academia and among the common people. Up until presently, Sanming City is the region with the largest number and the greatest variety of Fujian earthen fortresses.

Earthen fortresses are scattered in various areas of Sanming. However, there are only 50 earthen fortresses preserved well, most of which are situated in Datian, Youxi, Yong'an, Shaxian and etc...

Most of the earthen fortresses in Datian are located not far away from each other, in a large diversity and with various structures. Now there are altogether seven earthen fortresses listed in the 7th Batch of State Protected Historic Site, all of which are located in Datian. They were ranked among the top-level architectures for their features, systematicness and exquisiteness. Most of earthen fortresses in Shaxian are in brick-earth-wood structure, with the complete living facility; most of them are located not far away from each other, with their representative being Shuimei Earthen Fortress. The feature of Youxi Earthen Fortress is that most of them are in a large scale, with high stairs and many platforms; there are also many earthen houses, earthen buildings and earthen residences transformed from defensive earthen fortresses. Youxi earthen fortresses are in complex structures with sumptuous decorations, among which exquisite earthen fortresses sprang up one after another. Yong'an earthen fortresses are in delicate structures, with unique exterior appearance and interior decorations.

There were also earthen fortresses in Qingliu, Jiangle, Ninghua, Sanyuan and other counties before. But they were in a small number, and not preserved well. Kanhou Earthen Fortress in Jiangle and Songqing Earthen Fortress in Sanyuan are consummate architectures which is rarely seen.

芳联堡全景／Entire scenery of Fanglian Earthen Fortress

## 芳联堡（大田）

位于大田县均溪镇许思坑村，土堡坐落在山间河谷地带的山坡边，占地面积3350平方米，建筑面积5500平方米。该堡由当地张氏先祖始建于清朝嘉庆十一年（1806年），历时五年建成。芳联堡所在地三面环山，清溪环绕，堡墙为三合土打制而成，土堡兼有府第式建筑的特点，设计以人为本，适合居住，堡内专设鸽子笼，以备通讯之用。芳联堡为第七批国家级文物保护单位。

## Fanglian Earthen Fortress (Datian)

Fanglian Earthen Fortress is located in Xusikeng Village, Junxi Town, Datian County. Built down the hillside of a river valley, it covers an area of 3350 square meters and a gross floor area of 5500 square meters. It took a five-year effort of the ancestor of Zhang family clan to complete the construction which started in the 11th year during the rein of Emperor Jiaqing in Qing Dynasty (1806 AD). Surrounded by mountains on three sides, Fanglian Earthen Fortress is endowed with a crystal-clear stream running around it. The walls of the earthen fortress are made up of lime, clay and sand. Bearing the feature of a mansion, the fortress was designed according to people-centered principles, and thus suitable for living. There are also pigeon cages inside the fortress for communication. The fortress was listed in the 7th Batch of State Protected Historic Site.

三层碉式角楼，双楼错位重叠/Three-storey fort-type turret, twin building overlapping with each other and well-proportioned

坚固的堡墙，狭窄的堡门，紧闭的窗户，全是为了防御/Solid walls, narrow gate, closed windows, all for defense

堡内，生活气息浓郁／The fortress with a vigorous living atmosphere

后花台水井、跑马道、走廊／Well in the back flower stand, racing course, corridor

土堡内的农具／Agricultural implements in the earthen fortress

瓦上风景，芳联堡彩绘／The beauty in the tile, colored drawing in Fanglian Earthen Fortress

精美石雕／Exquisite stone sculptures

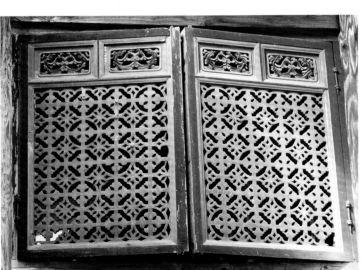

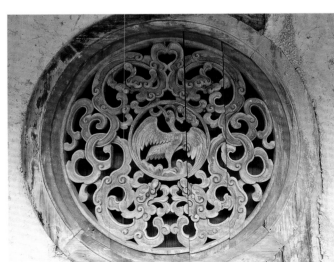

精美木雕/Exquisite wood sculptures

精美木雕／Exquisite wood sculptures

窗之风景，芳联堡内各式各样的窗／The beauty in the windows, various windows in Fanglian Earthen Fortress

## 安良堡（大田）

　　位于大田县桃源镇东坂村湖丘头自然村，坐落在山坡下，占地面积1500平方米，建筑面积1250平方米。安良堡由当地熊氏先祖始建于清朝嘉庆十一年（1806年），历时五年建成。安良堡处于群山环抱中，防御设计独特，建筑台基落差极大，高达14米，所有的堂屋依山势而建，人到顶端包房，如处空中楼阁。土堡建成之后，几遭兵匪围困，均安然无恙。安良堡为第七批国家级文物保护单位。

牢固的堡门／Solid gate

### Anliang Earthen Fortress (Datian)

　　Anliang Earthen Fortress is located in Huqiutou Unincorporated Village, Dongban Village, Taoyuan Town, Datian County. Built at the foot of a hill, it covers an area of 1500 square meters and a gross floor area of 1250 square meters. The ancestor of the local Xiong family clan built the architecture in the 11th year during the rein of Emperor Jiaqing in Qing Dynasty (1806) and used five years to complete the project. Tucked away among mountains, Anliang Earthen Fortress is featured by its special defensive designs, with a large drop height of 14 meters between the platforms. All the central rooms are built down the hillside. If you climb to the cabin on the top floor, you will feel like standing in an air-castle. After its completion, the earthen fortress was besieged by soldiers and brigands several times, and yet remained intact. Anliang Earthen Fortress was listed in the 7th Batch of State Protected Historic Site.

安良堡地理位置绝佳，为传统风水学中藏风藏水聚气生财之地／Located in an excellent geographical position, Anliang Earthen Fortress is the place which is blessed with the good fortune and wealth and sheltered from wind and storm according to traditional Chinese Feng Shui Theory

安良堡下堂、厢房／Hall of Anliang Earthen Fortress,wing-room

安良堡落差大，站在高处，视野极佳／Anliang Earthen Fortress is located in a high elevation. with a big drop height between different buildings,overlooking from the high fortress, one can enjoy a good view

如阶梯般排列的墙上廊屋／Rooms above the walls ranged in the ascending order

跑马道、传统农具／Racing course, traditional agricultural implements

安良堡墙体逐渐向上，共16级，埋入墙体的杉木桩颇具视觉冲击力／Walls of Anliang Earthen Fortress ranged in the ascending order, altogether 16 levels; the timber piles made up of Chinese fir embedded in the walls are eye-striking

琵琶堡外景／Outdoor scene of Pipa Earthen Fortress

牢固的堡门／Solid gate

## 琵琶堡（大田）

　　位于大田县建设镇建国村澄江自然村，土堡处在村中一座相对独立的山冈上，海拔高度612米，占地面积2000平方米，建筑面积1600平方米，为当地游氏先祖始建于明朝洪武初年。土堡基址形如山龟，外观又像琵琶。琵琶堡目前已无人居住。土堡将传统的风水理念、音乐理念融进设计与构筑之中。琵琶堡为第七批国家级文物保护单位。

## Pipa Earthen Fortress (Datian)

Pipa Earthen Fortress is located in Chengjiang Unincorporated Village, Jianguo Village, Jianshe Town, Datian Couty. Reposing in a relatively distinct hilltop in the village, it covers an area of 2000 square meters and a gross floor area of 1600 square meters, at an altitude of 612 meters above seal level. The ancestors of the local You family clan built the architecture in the early period during the rein of Emperor Hongwu in Ming Dynasty. The base of the earthen fortress resembles a turtle while the appearance of the fortress resembles a pipa, a plucked string instrument with a fretted fingerboard. Pipa Earthen Fortress now houses no residents. The design and structure of the earthen fortresses integrate the traditional geomancy and musical theories, which is bodied forth in the process of construction. Pipa Earthen Fortress listed in the 7th Batch of State Protected Historic Site.

琵琶堡，其外形如小龟，周边众多小山包势如"金蛇戏龟"，土堡周边均是陡坡，易守难攻/Pipa Earthen Fortress resembles a little turtle, with numerous surrounding hills – the entire scenery is like "golden snake playing with a turtle". The surrounding area of the earthen fortress is precipitous, easy to defend but hard to attack

堡内建筑尚存，但已无人居住／The interior structure of the fortress is still preserved, but it now houses no residents

人去楼空的琵琶堡/Bipa Earthen Fortress with no residents

跑马道，上有廊屋遮护／Racing course, sheltered from rooms above

潭城堡外景／Outdoor scene of Tancheng Earthen Fortress

## 潭城堡（大田）

　　位于大田县广平镇栋仁村，土堡位于水田中，占地面积2600平方米，建筑面积2100平方米。土堡由当地郑氏先祖始建于明朝万历年间，因建在有两处深潭的铭溪边，故而得名。潭城堡环境优美，是少见的圆形土堡，土堡在20世纪80年代因村部扩建遭到部分损坏。

## Tancheng Earthen Fortress (Datian)

　　Tancheng Earthen Fortress is located in Dongren Village, Guangping Town, Datian County. Reposing in a paddy field, it covers an area of 2600 square meters and a gross floor area of 2100 square meters. The earthen fortress was built by the ancestor of Zheng family clan during the rein of Wanli in Ming Dynasty. It was named due to its location near Ming River which contains two deep pools (Tan means deep pools in Chinese). Tancheng Earthen Fortress as a round fortress (which is rarely seen) is endowed with a beautiful environment. In 1980s, part of the fortress was damaged as a new addition was built to it.

潭城堡宽阔的跑马道／Wide racing course in Tancheng Earthen Fortress

绍恢堡全景／Entire scenery of Shaohui Earthen Fortress

## 绍恢堡（大田）

位于大田县广平镇万宅村，土堡建在山坡边，坐西南向东北，占地面积3200平方米，建筑面积2500平方米。绍恢堡是一座兼具府第式、五凤楼、围龙屋特点的防御性建筑，为当地余氏先祖余新权始建于清朝光绪十一年（1885年），土堡内装饰精美，木雕、彩绘、灰塑等技法娴熟，多为精品。2013年，绍恢堡被列入第七批国家级文物保护单位。

## Shaohui Earthen Fortress (Datian)

Shaohui Earthen Fortress is located in Wanzhai Village, Guangping Town, Datian County. Built down the hillside, it faces northeast with an area of 3200 square meters and a gross floor area of 2500 square meters. The fortress combines defensive functions and the features of buildings such as residence, Phoenix Building and Hakka Walled House. Yu Xinquan, the ancestor of the local Yu family clan built the fortress in the 11th year during the rein of Emperor Guangxu in Qing Dynasty (1885 AD). The interior decorations are exquisite, most of which are at top level, employing wood-carving skills, colored drawing, lime modeling and relevant skills. In 2013, Shaohui Earthen Fortress was listed in the 7th Batch of State Protected Historic Site.

绍恢堡已无人居住，由土堡后人共同管理／Shaohui Earthen Fortress now houses no residents and is managed by the posterity of the earthen fortress together

绍恢堡围墙不高，但坚实厚重，基础部分用大块毛石堆砌／The walls of Shaohui Earthen Fortress are not high but solid and heavy. Its foundation is piled up by the large block stones

绍恢堡正堂、堡门、石磨／Central Hall of Shaohui Earthen Fortress, gate, stone mill

光裕堡全景／Entire scenery of Guangyu Earthen Fortress

## 光裕堡（大田）

位于大田县广平镇万筹村，土堡建在水田中，占地面积近3000平方米，建筑面积约4500平方米。土堡前方后圆，为当地郑氏先祖郑朝裘始建于清朝乾隆年间。光裕堡为第七批国家级文物保护单位。

## Guangyu Earthen Fortress (Datian)

Guangyu Earthen Fortress is located in Wanchou Village, Guangping Town, Datian County. Built in a paddy field, it covers an area of almost 3000 square meters and a gross floor area of about 4500 square meters. The fortress has a square-faced front and round-faced back. Zheng Chaoqiu, the ancestor of the local Zheng family clan built it during the rein of Emperore Qianlong in Qing Dynasty. Guangyu Earthen Fortress was listed in the 7th Batch of State Protected Historic Site.

俯瞰光裕堡／Overlooking from Guangyu Earthen Fortress

厚重的堡门、土堡建在水田中都是为了更好地防御／Heavy gate, the earthen fortress is built in the paddy field, which is better for defense

光裕堡内建筑讲究中轴线的布局，正堂尤为气派／The layout of the interior structure of Guangyu Earthen Fortress is featured by structures arranged along the central axis and a porticalarly magnificent central hall

光裕堡内尚有人居住／Guangyu Earthen Fortress now still houses some residents

精美的彩绘，全是故事/Exquisite colored drawings, all of which are telling their own stories and legends

雨梗墙上的精美彩绘／Exquisite colored drawings in Yugeng Walls

架梁上的精美木雕／Exquisite wood sculptures on roof beams

窗户风景，纹窗上的透雕／The beauty of windows, hollowed-out sculptures in the windows

凤阳堡全景／Entire scenery of Fengyang Earthen Fortress

## 凤阳堡（大田）

　　位于大田济阳乡济中村，土堡建在水田中，占地面积2500平方米，建筑面积2600平方米。凤阳堡由当地涂氏始建于清朝乾隆年间，土堡不设碉式角楼，但堡墙高大，跑马道宽敞。凤阳堡堡墙上的彩绘为土堡中少见，堡内已无人居住，但该堡环境风貌、原始状况保存较好。

## Fengyang Earthen Fortress (Datian)

Fengyang Earthen Fortress is located in Jizhong Village, Jiyang Township, Datian. Built in a paddy field, it covers an area of 2500 square meters and a gross floor area of 2600 square meters. The local Xu family clan built the fortress during the rein of Emperor Qianlong in Qing Dynasty. There are no fort-type turrets in the fortress, but the walls are towering and the racing course is wide inside it. The colored drawings in the walls of the fortress are rarely seen. Now the fortress houses no residents. However, the environment and original structures are preserved well.

凤阳堡位于水田中，易守难攻/Located in a paddy field, Fengyang Earthen Fortress is easy to defend and hard to attack

凤阳堡侧门、正门/Side entrance of Fengyang Earthen Fortress, main entrance of Fengyang Earthen Fortress

凤阳堡内超大空坪和跑马道／Super large ground and racing course in Fengyang Earthen Fortress

泰安堡外景／outdoor scene of Tai'an Earthen Fortress

## 泰安堡（大田）

　　位于大田县太华镇小华村，土堡占地面积850平方米，建筑面积2100平方米。土堡为当地林氏先祖始建于清朝咸丰年间，几经修葺，几百年来庇佑着小华村村民。泰安堡堡墙坚固高峻，而且注重立面效果，七层的碉式角楼显示土堡恢宏的气势。2013年，泰安堡被列入第七批国家级文物保护单位。

## Tai'an Earthen Fortress (Datian)

　　Tai'an Earthen Fortress is located in Xiaohua Village, Taihua Town, Datian County. The fortress covers an area of 850 square meters and a gross floor area of 2100 square meters. The ancestor of the local Lin family clan built the fortress during the rein of Emperor Xianfeng in Qing Dynasty. It has been refurnished several times, for centuries, it offered a haven for villagers of Xiaohua Village. The walls of Tai'an Earthen Fortress are substantial and towering, with effects of façade being stressed. The seven-storey fort-type turret set off the magnificence of the fortress. In 2013, Tian Earthen Fortress was listed in the 7th Batch of State Protected Historic Site.

远眺泰安堡／Looking at Tai'an Earthen Fortress from far

碉式角楼、泰安堡内三层楼建筑／Fort-type turret, three-storey building in Tai'an Earthen Fortress

瑞庆堡正门／Main entrance of Ruiqing Earthen Fortress

## 瑞庆堡（尤溪）

又名邱家堡围，位于尤溪县台溪乡书京村31号，依山而建，坐落在水田中，坐西南向东北，前方后圆，占地面积2500平方米，建筑面积2300平方米。堡门石门额上题刻"紫气东来"以及落款"大清光绪六年"显示该堡落成时间为1880年的春天。瑞庆堡兼具土堡和围龙屋等建筑元素，堡内设有书院，并引隐蔽山泉水入堡，兼具居住和防御功能。此外，堡内间或种植桃、柿子等果树，生活情趣盎然。

## Ruiqing Earthen Fortress (Youxi)

Ruiqing Earthen Fortress, also known as Qiujia Walled Fortress, is located in No.31, Shujing Village, Taixi Township, Youxi County. Built down the hillside within a paddy field, it faces northeast with a square-faced front and round-faced back, covering an area of 2500 square meters and a gross floor area of 2300 square meters. The stone plague above the gate of the fortress were carved with the Chinese characters of "Auspicious Air Coming from the East" and the date "The 6th Year during the rein of Emperor Guangxu in Qing Dynasty", which reveals the date of completion – the spring of 1880 AD. Combining the architectural features of the earthen structure and Hakka Walled Village, the builders have built an academy of classical learning and drew the spring water through a secrete channel into the fortress, making the whole structure suitable for residing and defense. Furthermore, peach trees and permission are planted alternately, giving this area a joyous taste of life.

瑞庆堡，建在山坡下水田边／Ruiqing Earthen Fortress is built in a paddy field down the hillside

瑞庆堡主堂／Main hall of Ruiqing Earthen Fortress

阶梯状跑马道，外为台阶，内为坡道／Terraced racing course surrounded by staircases outside, with ramps inside

柱础上的精美石雕和雨梗墙上的彩绘／Exquisite stone sculptures in pillar bases, colored drawings in Yugeng Walls

光裕堡外景／Outdoor scene of Guangyu Earthen Fortress

## 光裕堡（尤溪）

又名天六土堡，与瑞庆堡相隔不远，位于尤溪县台溪乡书京村36号，堪称书京村"双子堡"，也一同被列入省级文物保护单位。光裕堡依山而建，坐西向东，前方后圆，占地面积2600平方米，建筑面积2200平方米。光裕堡依山势分四级台阶构建，前后落差15米，气势壮观。据当地邱氏族谱记载，光裕堡为先祖邱长厚于清朝道光年间，率子孙而建。堡内门洞题刻"宽厚流风""道光三十年梅月吉旦"则表明光裕堡落成时间为1850年。光裕堡气势恢宏，构思精巧，为不可多得的土堡精品。

## Guangyu Earthen Fortress (Youxi)

Guangyu Earthen Fortress, also known as Tianliu Earthen Fortress, stood not far from Ruiqing Earthen Fortress. Located in No.36, Shujing Village, Taixi Township, Youxi County, it is well-known as "Shuangzi Earthen Fortresses" with Ruiqing Earthen Fortress (the two fortresses are both listed as the cultural relic protection unit at provincial level). Reposing alongside a hill, it faces east with a square-faced front and round-faced back, covering an area of 2600 square meters and a gross floor area of 2200 square meters. Guangyu Earthen Fortress is built on four levels of stairs to fit in the mountain alongside, with a drop height of 15 meters between the top level and the ground level, creating an imposing appearance. According to the records of the pedigree of Qiu family clan, the ancestor named Qiu Changhou built it with his offspring during the rein of Emperor Daoguang in Qing Dynasty. Above the doorway of the fortress, it is carved with the Chinese characters of "Carrying forward Generosity as a Family Tradition" and the date "The 1st Day of April in Lunar Calendar in the 30th year during the rein of Emperor Daoguang", which indicates that the date of completion is 1850 AD. Standing solemn and majestic, it boasts of ingenuity and exquisiteness, completely deserving the reputation of the consummate earthen fortress.

壁垒森严的堡门、过道／Strongly fortified gate,passageway

光裕堡主堂／Main hall of Guangyu Earthen Fortress

堡内生活场景／Scenes of life in the fortress

茂荆堡全景／Entire scenery of Maojing Earthen Fortress

## 茂荆堡（尤溪）

又名盖竹堡，位于尤溪县台溪乡盖竹村乌岩垄内一处相对独立的山坡上，土堡坐东北向西南，占地面积2600多平方米，建筑面积3000多平方米。茂荆堡气势恢宏，要靠近土堡，必须经过1千米的弯曲山道，在接近土堡的山垄两边各有天然钟鼓石，起示警作用。茂荆堡由陈氏先祖始建于清朝光绪八年（1882年），历时三年完工。

## Maojing Earthen Fortress (Youxi)

Maojing Earthen Fortress, also known as Gaizhu Earthen Fortress, is situated on a distinct hill within Wuyuan Ridge, Gaizhu Village, Taixi Township, Youxi County. Facing southeast, it covers an area of over 2600 square meters and a gross floor area of above 3000 square meters. Maojing Earthen Fortress is a magnificent architecture. To approach it, one has to trudge for one mile along a sinuous path. Along the ridge close to the fortress, there are natural Zhonggu stones (stones chiming like drum or bell when struck) of various types, playing the function of warning. Maojing Earthen Fortress was built by the ancestors of Chen family clan in the 8th year during the rein of Emperor Guangxu in the Qing Dynasty, taking three years to complete in toto.

茂荆堡正门／Main entrance of Maojing Earthen Fortress

茂荆堡主堂、双重天井和厢房／Central hall of Maojing Earthen, double skylight and wing-rooms

阶梯状的跑马道，相传土堡有108间房间／Terraced racing course; legend goes that there are 108 rooms in the earthen fortress

过道／Passageway

梁上精美木雕、时代印记／Exquisite wood sculptures on the beams, symbols of the time

耕读之家／A family embracing farming and reading

聚奎堡外景／Outdoor scene of Jukui Earthen Fortress

## 聚奎堡（尤溪）

位于尤溪县中仙乡西华村51号，该堡坐西向东，始建于清朝乾隆十九年（1754年），因该堡历代文人辈出，奎星点点故得名聚奎堡。土堡总建筑面积6552平方米，选址和设计均别出心裁，建筑依地势而建，集居住生活和防御为一体。历史上，聚奎堡几建几废，现存建筑为清朝光绪十四年（1889年）复建，融合了福州和闽中的建筑元素。聚奎堡为福建土堡少有的精美之作，2001年，聚奎堡被列入福建省第五批省级文物保护单位。

## Jukui Earthen Fortress (Youxi)

Jukui Earthen Fortress is situated in No.51, Xihua Village, Zhongxian Township, Youxi County. It was built in the 19th year during the rein of Emperor Qianlong in Qing Dynasty (1754 AD). It became known as Jukui Earthen Fortress due to a galaxy of talents hailing from the fortress as it literally means talented people coming forth in a large number in Chinese. Facing east, the fortress covers a gross floor area of 6552 square meters. Its selection of location and design is off the beaten track. Built down the hillside, the architecture combines the function of living and defense. In history, Jukui Earthen Fortress went through dilapidation and renovation several times. The presently conserved structure was refurnished in the 14th year during the rein of Emperor Guangxu in Qing Dynasty (1889 AD), thus integrating the elements of architectures in Fuzhou and the middle Fujian. Jukui Earthen Fortress is a rare outstanding work among the earthen fortresses in Fujian province. In 2001, Jukui Earthen Fortress was listed as one of the 5th Batch of Cultural Relic Protection Unit of Fujian Province.

聚奎堡正门／Main entrance of Jukui Earthen Fortress

厅堂内的神位／Memorial tablet in a hall

时代的标语／Slogans of an era

楼梯、过道、防守斗窗、石磨、石臼／Staircase,passageway,Bucket-type windows for defense,stone mill,stone mortar

农闲季节，天晴好晒谷／Slack farming season, it is better to dry grain in a fine day

当地特产／Products with local flavors

钟祥堡全景／Entire scenery of Zhongxiang Earthen Fortress

寂寞美人靠／Back-rest chair for lonely beauties

## 钟祥堡（尤溪）

又称池家古堡，位于尤溪县中仙乡中仙村。土堡原坐落于山坡边水田中，随着城镇化的发展，钟祥堡已经处在现代建筑的包围之中。土堡始建于清朝雍正初年，民国初年重修，土堡坐东向西，占地面积2000平方米，建筑面积1800平方米，堡楼结合，外形似方楼，但堡外挖有护堡溪，内有跑马道、碉式角楼等防御措施。钟祥堡的居民基本已经外迁在堡外建房，目前仅一户人家住在堡内。

## Zhongxiang Earthen Fortress (Youxi)

Zhongxiang Earthen Fortress, also known as Chijia Ancient Fortress, is located in Zhongxian Village, Zhongxian Township, Youxiu County. Formally lying within the paddy field alongside a hill, it is now surrounded by the modern architectures due to the urbanization drive. The fortress was built in the early years during the rein of Emperor Yongzheng and revamped in the early period of ROC. Facing west, it covers an area of 2000 square meters and a gross floor area of 1800 square meters. Combining the features of a fortress and a mansion, it resembles the Fanglou (a square building in China). A moat runs around the fortress, within which there is a race course and a fort-type turret, which residents used with other facilities for defense. Now most of its residents had moved outside. Up until presently, only one family still to live inside the fortress.

土堡成为杂物堆放地/Earthen fortress becoming a dumping ground for all the crap

土堡处在现代建筑的包围中/The earthen fortress surrounded by modern architectures

最后的土堡人家／The last family in the earthen fortress

## 郑氏土堡（尤溪）

位于中仙乡苏峰村村部旁，始建于清朝，郑氏土堡占地面积约1200平方米，建筑面积1800平方米。郑氏土堡建在水田中，与相邻的石头桥堡相隔仅仅6米，均为当地郑氏宗亲合建。目前两个土堡均已无人居住，石头桥堡破坏严重，部分墙体已经坍塌。

## Zheng Family Earthen Fortress (Youxi)

The fortress is located alongside Sufeng Village, Zhongxian Township. Built in Qing Dynasty, it covers an area of about 1200 square meters and a gross floor area of 1800 square meters. Reposing in a paddy field, it is just six meters away from the Stone Bridge Earthen Fortress in the vicinity, which were both built by the Zheng family clan. Now there are residents within the two fortresses. In severe conditions, parts of the walls of Stone Bridge Earthen Fortress have already collapsed.

郑氏土堡外景／Outdoor scene of Zheng Family Earthen Fortress

破坏严重的土堡／The earthen fortress severely damaged

德芳堡外景／Outdoor scene of Defang Earthen Fortress

土堡已成村部所在地／The earthen fortress which has become the office area of a village government

## 德芳堡（尤溪）

位于坂面镇京口村村部的山溪边，土堡坐西向东，占地面积3560平方米，建筑面积2560平方米。京口村地处大山中，山清水秀，始建于清末民初的德芳堡格外醒目。土堡对角设碉式角楼，相当壮观，堡内马头墙极具福州民居建筑特点。当地村民已经着手开发旅游，以促进土堡的保护。

## Defang Earthen Fortress (Youxi)

Defang Earthen Fortress is located in the mountain creek of Jingkou Village, Banmian Town. Facing east, it covers an area of 3560 square meters and a gross floor area of 2560 square meters. Tucked away among the mountains, Jingkou Village is endowed with beautiful mountains and crystal-clear water. Located in the village, Defang Earthen Fortress is a remarkable architecture built at the end of Qing Dynasty and the early phase of ROC. Along the diagonal line of the fortress, a fort-type turret was built – a rather imposing structure. Besides, the Matou Wall (a type of fireproofing wall in ancient China) within the fortress is a characteristic structure in the Fuzhou civil dwellings. Presently, local villagers have carried out tourist development programs to try to protect the fortress through development.

德芳堡已成村部所在地，在利用中被保护/Defang Earthen Fortress has become the office area of the village government, preserved while still at use

堡内建筑／Interior structures of the earthen fortress

精美的柱础／Exquisite column bases

大福圳平面呈两个长方形重叠的"7"字/Dafuzhen resembles seven rectangle overlapping characters in the plane plan

堡门/Gate

## 大福圳（尤溪）

　　大福圳，是具有土堡防御元素的庄园式建筑，位于尤溪县梅仙镇坪寨村上洋一号。大福圳坐北向南，占地面积8000多平方米，建筑面积7000多平方米，由萧氏先祖萧惠卿于清朝光绪元年（1875年）始建，历经十年而成。大福圳是尤溪目前现存最大的带有防御性古建筑。

---

## Dafuzhen (Youxi)

　　Dafuzhen is a structure with defending features of the fortress and style of a villa. It is located in No.1, Shanyang, Pingzhai Village, Meixian Town, Youxi County. Facing south, it covers an area of above 8000 square meters and a gross floor area of over 7000 square meters. Started to be built by the ancestor of Xiao family clan, Xiao Huiqing, in the first year during the rein of Emperor Guangxu (1875 AD), it took a decade to be completed. Up until presently, Dafuzhen is the largest ancient architecture with defending elements preserved in Youxi.

厅堂、寂寞美人靠、门冈／Hall, back-rest chair for lonely beauties, bars

双层天井／Two-level skylights

时代的标语／Slogans of an era

"福"字、纹窗、隔窗透雕／The character of "Fortune", windows, hollowed-out sculptures in windows

幽深的走道／Deep and far-reaching corridor

精美的彩绘／Exquisite colored drawings

精美的彩绘/Exquisite colored drawings

莲花堡碉式角楼／Fort-type turret of Lotus Earthen Fortress

## 莲花堡（尤溪）

　　位于尤溪县梅仙镇汶潭村，该堡坐东朝西，占地面积约4000平方米，现存的建筑面积约980平方米，由曾任武平训导的周之楫始建于清朝康熙三年（1695年）。莲花堡因所处地名"莲花池"而得名，堡内建筑曾遭到损毁。莲花堡四周修有护堡沟壕，壕面宽达7米，深约2.5米，为少有的防御天然屏障。莲花堡人才辈出，曾出过清代武探花周熙光等名人。

### Lotus Earthen Fortress (Youxi)

　　Lotus Earthen Fortress is located in Wentan Village, Meixian Town, Youxi County. Facing west, it covers an area of about 4000 square meters. The area now preserved is about 980 square meters. Built in the 3rd year during the rein of Emperor Kangxi in Qing Dynasty by Zhou Zhiji, a formal Xundao (an official instructor appointed by the government in ancient China) of Wuping, it was named for its location – Lotus Pond. The structures within it have been damaged. A moat runs around the fortress, about 7 meters in width and about 2.5 meters in depth, - setting up a rare natural line of defense. Lotus Earthen Fortress is the cradle of many talents, e.g., Zhou Xiguang, Number 3 in the imperial military art examination in Qing Dynasty.

俯瞰莲花堡／A bird's view of Lotus Earthen Fortress

莲花堡堡门／Gate of Lotus Earthen Fortress

土堡内的空坪／An empty ground in the earthen fortress

莲花堡内建筑，上为住房，下为仓库/Architectures inside the Lotus Earthen Fortress, with the above level being rooms and the lower level being storage house

厅堂内的精美木雕/Hall, Exquisite wood sculptures

厚重的堡墙/Strongly fortified gate

跑马道／Racing course

升平堡全景／Entire scenery of Shengping Earthen Fortress

## 升平堡（尤溪）

　　位于尤溪县新阳镇上地村，升平堡始建于清朝，坐北向南，占地面积约2100平方米，建筑面积1500平方米。土堡坐落在群山合围的一座相对独立的山冈上，多台基，高落差，但探寻之路相当艰巨，目前堡内已无人居住，堡外荒草丛生，堡内设施齐全，但也面临损毁的危险。

### Shengping Earthen Fortress (Youxi)

Shenping Earthen Fortress is located in Shangdi Village, Xinyang Town, Youxi County. Firstly built in Qing Dynasty, it faces south with an area of about 2100 square meters and a gross floor area of 1500 square meters. Reposing in a distinct hilltop surrounded by mountains, it has many stylobates with a large drop height, making it rather a tough task to approach the fortress. Now there are no residents within the fortress. Outside the fortress, it is covered with weeds. But the facilities inside is complete, though facing the danger of damage.

升平堡堡门／Gate of Shengping Earthen Fortress

人去堡空／An empty earthen fortress

无人居住的土堡，农具尚存，依稀可以想象当年的热闹/An earthen fortress now houses no residents, with agricultural implements left. One can imagine the noisy scenes of its bygone days

## 公馆峡（尤溪）

位于尤溪县新阳镇双鲤村，为尤溪具有土堡防御元素的庄园性建筑，当地人称卢公馆。公馆峡由福建军阀卢兴邦于1922年兴建，该建筑坐北向南，占地面积3150平方米，建筑面积2194平方米。公馆峡雄伟壮观，布局合理，民居内部有大量精美的装饰，集居住性和防御性于一体。已经被列为福建省级重点文物保护单位。

### Gongguanxia (Youxi)

Gongguanxia is located in Shuangli Village, Xinyang Town, Youxi County. It is a villa combining the defending elements of earthen fortresses in Youxi County, known as Lu Mansion among local folks. Built in 1922 by Lu Xingbang, a warlord in Fujian, it faces south with an area of 3150 square meters and a gross floor area of 2194 square meters. Standing imposing and majestic, Guangguanxia has a proper layout. Within the architecture, there are a large number of exquisite decorations, combining the features of living and defense. Now it has already been listed as Key Cultural Relic Protection Unit of Fujian Province.

公馆峡正门／Main entrance of Gongguanxia

公馆峡全景／Entire scenery of Gongguanxia

中堂内悬挂蒋介石题匾／Central hall with a plague inscribed tith words of Chiang Kai-shek

姊妹楼，相传为卢家小姐读书女红之所／Sisters' Building; it is said that it was once a place the ladies of Lu family clan read and did needlework

卢公馆已列为福建省级重点文物保护单位，得到妥善保护／Lugongguan has been listed as a cultural protection site at provincial level, and is well preserved

双元堡外景／Outdoor scene of Shuangyuan Earthen Fortress

双元堡侧门，上刻"磬安"／Side door of Shuangyuan Earthen Fortress, with the characters of "Pan'an" inscribed

## 双元堡（沙县）

　　位于沙县凤岗街道水美村大泷山地的山坡边，坐西向东，占地面积6500平方米，建筑面积5372平方米。始建于清朝道光年间，清朝同治元年（1862年）完工。双元堡所处的水美土堡群由三座土堡组成，均为张氏先祖所建，双元堡是其中规模最大、气势最恢宏的一座。堡内建筑保存完好，内设慎修堂，由三进九厅十八井的建筑所组成，可供千人居住，目前堡内仅有几户人家居住。

## Shuangyuan Earthen Fortress (Sha County)

It is located alongside a hill of Dalong Mountainous Region of Shuimei Village, Fenggang Subdistrict, Sha County. Facing east, it covers an area of 6500 square meters and a gross floor area of 5372 square meters. Firstly built during the rein of Emperor Daoguang in Qing Dynasty, it was completed in the first year during the rein of Emperor Tongzhi (1862 AD). Among the three earthen fortresses consisting Shuimei Earthen Fortress Cluster, which were all built by the ancestors of Zhang family clan, Shuangyuan Earthen Fortress is the largest and most magnificent one. The structures within the fortress are preserved well with Shenxiu Hall built inside. Made up of 9 halls and 18 courtyards in 3 arrays, it can house a thousand persons. Now there are only several households living within the fortress.

双元堡正门，门额为"奠厥攸居"，出自《尚书》／Main entrance of Shuangyuan Earthen Fortress, with "Mojue Youju" (Place of Settlement) inscribed in the horizontal board above the gate, quoted from "Book of History"

双元堡侧门，上刻"巩固"／Side door of Shuangyuan Earthen Fortress

土堡过道，寂寞锁清秋／Passageway of an earthen fortress, locked away in a lonely and drear autumn

厅堂／Hall

水缸防火／Water vat, precautions to prevent fire

堡内，生活气息浓郁／Interior structures of the fortress with a vigorous living atmosphere

土堡人家／Households living in the earthen fortress

双兴堡全景／Entire scenery of Shuangxing Earthen Fortress

双兴堡侧门／Side door of Shuangxing Earthen Fortress

## 双兴堡（沙县）

　　位于沙县凤岗街道水美村秋竹林山边，坐南向北，占地面积4300平方米，建筑面积5065平方米。始建于清朝道光年间，清朝咸丰年间完工。堡内设有致美堂，各种建筑完整。前堡墙大部分被拆。

---

## Shuangxing Earthen Fortress (Sha County)

Shuangxing Earthen Fortress is located alongside a hill next to a bamboo forest of Shuimei Village, Fenggang Sub-district, Sha County. Facing north, it covers an area of 4300 square meters and a gross floor area of 5065 square meters. Built during the rein of Emperor Daoguang in Qing Dynasty, it was completed during the rein of Emperor Xianfeng. Within the fortress, there is Zhimei Hall and well preserved structures of various types. Most of the walls in the front of the fortress were demolished.

堡内，生活气息浓郁／Interior structures of the fortress with a vigorous living atmosphere

致美堂内的神像、祈福对联／Faith and praying in Zhimei Hall

土堡人家，市井烟火/Households in the earthen fortress, life of ordinary people

安贞堡正门／Main entrance of Anzhen
Earthen Fortress

## 安贞堡（永安）

也称池贯城，位于永安市槐南乡洋头村村北的大山余脉上，坐西向东，占地面积8500平方米，建筑面积6700平方米。安贞堡由池氏先祖池占瑞、池云龙父子于清朝光绪十一年（1885年）始建，清朝光绪二十四年（1898年）竣工，前后十四年，工程浩大。堡内现有房间300多个，书房、仓库、过厅、碉式角楼等一应俱全，装饰相当精美奢华，是福建乃至全国最大的土堡。安贞堡也是名气最大、最早为人所熟知的土堡，是第五批全国重点文物保护单位。

### Anzhen Earthen Fortress (Yong'an)

Anzhen Earthen Fortress, also known as Chiguangcheng, is located in the range of the mountain to the north of Yangtou Village, Huainan Township, Yong'an City. It faces east with an area of 8500 square meters and a gross floor area of 6700 square meters. Anzhen Earthen Fortress was built by Chi Zhanrui and his son Chi Yunlong, the ancestors of Chi family clan in the 11th year during the rein of Emperor Guangxu in Qing Dynasty. Built in the 24th year during the rein of Emperor Guangxu (1898 AD), it is a gigantic project, taking a 14-year effort. The fortress consists of over 300 rooms, study, storage, gallery, fort-type turret and other facilities. It is decorated in exquisite and sumptuous style – by far, it is the largest fortress in Fujian and even in China. Anzhen Earthen Fortress is the most famous fortress, whose reputation was gained the earliest. It is also one of the 5th Batch of National Key Cultural Relic Protection Units.

安贞堡全景／Entire scenery of Anzhen Earthen Fortress

安贞堡内木雕、彩绘、灰塑均相当精美／Rather exquisite wood sculptures, colored drawings, and grey-model sculptures

安贞堡一进天井与回形扶楼／Skylight and building resembling the Chinese character of "Hui" of Anzhen Earthen Fortress

惟妙惟肖的灰塑动物／Life-like grey-model animal sculptures

历经百年的彩绘，色彩犹新／The colored drawings with a history of one hundred years, still looking new with its colors

雕梁画栋，金碧辉煌／Carved beams and painted rafters, resplendent and magnificent

安贞堡共360个房间，规模宏大／Altogether 360 rooms in Anzhen Earthen Fortress, in a gigantic scale

安贞堡内木雕精美，极具艺术价值／Exquisite wood sculptures in Anzhen Earthen Fortress of artistic value

层层叠叠，错落有致／Overlapping and well-proportioned

安贞堡内的透雕木窗，费时费工，精美异常／Windows with hollowed out sculptures of Anzhen Earthen Fortress, taking time and efforts to complete, and yet exhibiting an extremely exquisite appearance

壁画华丽精美／Exquisite wall paintings

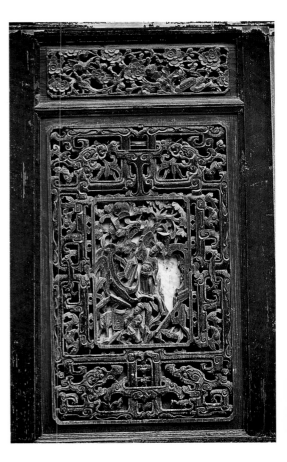

木雕装饰极尽繁复，华丽精美／Extremely complicated and exquisite wood sculptures

木雕装饰极尽繁复，华丽精美／Extremely complicated and exquisite wood sculptures

精美的石雕／Exquisite stone sculptures

### 复兴堡（永安）

　　位于永安市燕西街道文龙村50号，坐西向东，占地面积2800平方米，建筑面积2300平方米。土堡由余倬仪为首的当地余氏宗亲于清朝中晚期建造。复兴堡在抗战时期，曾作为重要的办公地点，历时七年，国民党台湾党部也在此驻扎过，属于重要的涉台文物。复兴堡，被列入第七批全国重点文物保护单位，目前得到妥善修缮，对外开放。

### Fuxing Earthen Fortress (Yong'an)

　　It is located in No.50, Wenlong Village, Yanxi Sub-district, Yong'an City. It faces east, covering an area of 2800 square meters and a gross floor area of 2300 square meters. Built in the medium and late period of Qing Dynasty by the local folks of Yu family clan headed by Yu Zhuoyi, Fuxing Earthen Fortress has once been an important office area for 7 years in the Anti-Japanese War. The Taiwan Party Committee of KMT was once located there, making it an important relic related to Taiwan. Listed as one of the 7th Batch of National Key Cultural Relic Protection Units, it has been well restored and open to the public.

复兴堡正门/Main entrance of Fuxing Earthen Fortress

修葺一新的复兴堡/Fuxing Earthen Fortress completely new after renovation

复兴堡中长条式天井／Strip-shaped skylight in Fuxing Earthen Fortress

经过修缮的复兴堡／Fuxing Earthen Fortress after renovation

抗战时期，复兴堡曾作为国民党台湾党部办公室，是重要的涉台文物／During the anti-Japanese war, Fuxing Earthen Fortress was once the office area of the party committee of KMT of Taiwan. So it is an important cultural relic related to Taiwan

铺砖的跑马道、厅堂／Racing course paved with bricks,hall

## 易安堡（永安）

又称堡中堡、黄白堡，位于永安洪田镇忠洛村丰溪自然村。该堡坐东北向西南，占地面积2400平方米，建筑面积3200平方米。易安堡原名易安堂，始建者为陈希岩，为防盗贼，陈高超在其父易安堂的基础上，扩堂为堡，于清朝道光二十三年（1843年）建成，即成为全村陈姓合族避难之所。如今，土堡已无人居住，堡内的木构建筑糟朽严重，亟待保护。

### Yi'an Earthen Fortress (Yong'an)

Yi'an Earthen Fortress is also known as Fortress within Fortress or Yellow-and-White Earthen Fortress. It is located in Fengxi Unincorporated Village, Zhongluo Village, Hongtian Town, Yong'an City. Facing southwest, it covers an area of 2400 square meters and a gross floor area of 3200 square meters. Formerly named as Yi'an Hall, it was built by Chen Xiyan to defend against bandits and thieves. His son Chen Gaochao expanded the hall into a fortress and completed the project in the 23rd year during the rein of Emperor Daoguang in Qing Dynasty (1843 AD), making it a haven for Chen family clan in the village. Nowadays, the fortress houses no residents with its severely damaged wooden structure, which requires an immediate preservation.

谷仓／Granary

田边的易安堡，又称黄白堡／Yi'an Earthen Fortress beside a paddy field, also known as Yellow and White Earthen Fortress

易安堡分两次建成，由白土堡（先建）、黄土堡（后建）组成／Yi'an Earthen Fortress was completed in two projects, consisted of White Earthen Fortress (firstly built) and Yellow Earthen Fortress (built later)

人去堡空、村民遗留的寿材／The fortress with no residents, coffins left by villagers

## 福临堡（永安）

位于永安市青水畲族乡过坑村，土堡坐西北向东南，占地面积2500平方米，建筑面积约1500平方米。福临堡的建造人为林仲易，于清朝乾隆五年（1740年）开始建造，用工精细，装饰华丽，福临堡得名来自正门的一对藏头联"福善从知天泽渥，临门遇见日精华"。堡内居民大多迁出，目前仅一户尚住在原地。

福临堡外景／Outdoor scene of Fulin Earthen Fortress

## Fulin Earthen Fortress (Yong'an)

Fulin Earthen Fortress is located in Guokeng Village, Qingshui She Ethnic Group Township, Yong'an City. Facing southeast, it covers an area of 2500 square meters and a gross floor area of about 1500 square meters. The builder of Fulin Earthen Fortress is Lin Zhongyi. Built in the 5th year during the rein of Emperor Qianlong (1740 AD), it used fine materials and splendent decorations. Fulin Earthen Fortress was named due to a couplet hanging above the front door, which writes that "Blessed with the grace of Heaven, basked in the essence of the sunlight". Most of the residents within the fortress have moved out, with only one household left.

福临堡全景／Entire scenery of Fulin Earthen Fortress

祖堂／Ancestor's hall

时光流转，斑驳的墙体见证岁月的风雨／The time elapsed, with mottled walls witnessing the vicissitudes of time

堡内景观，杂草丛生／The sceneries inside the earthen fortress, with weeds running riot

祖堂前檐廊柱梁上木雕和正堂梁上的木雕/Wood sculptures on the beams in porch columns of the eaves of the ancestor's hall, wood sculptures on the beams of the central hall

传统农具和谷仓/Traditional agricultural implements and granary

岗陵堡外景／Outdoor scene of Gangling Earthen Fortress

春花烂漫／Spring flowers in full bloom

## 岗陵堡（永安）

　　位于永安市青水畲族乡龙吴村官坑自然村东山脚下，坐东向西，占地面积2800平方米，建筑面积3500平方米。岗陵堡的建造者为官坑蔡氏先祖，始建于清朝康熙年间。1930年，军阀卢兴邦部袭掠官坑，全村人躲在岗陵堡内，方幸免于难。如今岗陵堡已无人居住，堡外是一大片的莴苣田，蓝天下，岗陵堡更显巍峨。

## Gangling Earthen Fortress (Yong'an)

Gangling Earthen Fortress is located at the root of Dong Mountain, Guankeng Unincorporated Village, Longwu Village, Qingshui She Ethnic Group Township, Yong'an City. Facing west, it covers an area of 2800 square meters and a gross floor area of 3500 square meters. Gangling Earthen Fortress was built by Cai family clan during the rein of Emperor Kangxi in Qing Dynasty. In 1930, when the warlord Lu Xingbang plundered Guangkeng, all the villagers hid within the Fortress and survived the disaster. Now Gangling Earthen Fortress houses no residents. Outside the fortress, a vast expanse of lettuce field reposes in the proximity. Under the blue canopy of heaven, Gangling Earthen Fortress stands more prodigious.

岗陵堡正门、门额上的楷体墨书"光风霁月"已模糊不清／Main entrance of Gangling Earthen Fortress, with blurred characters in regular script in the horizontal board – "Open and above board"

岗陵堡已无人居住，风流早被雨打风吹去／Gangling Earthen Fortress now houses no residents; its glories have eclipsed in the passing time

治元堡正门／Main entrance of Zhiyuan Earthen Fortress

## 治元堡（永安）

　　位于永安市青水畲族乡炉丘村，坐西向东，占地面积2100平方米，建筑面积1750平方米。治元堡位于田中，是由炉丘村罗氏家族和刘氏家族联合兴建的土堡，始建年代为清朝晚期。治元堡门前两边为长方形泮池，也是防御利器。历史上，治元堡曾是村子里的药店，目前土堡内仅有一人守护。

## Zhiyuan Earthen Fortress (Yong'an)

　　Zhiyuan Earthen Fortress is located in Luqiu Village, Qingshui She Ethnic Group Township, Yong'an City. Facing east, it covers an area of 2100 square meters and a gross floor area of 1750 square meters. Reposing in a field now, it was co-built by Luo family clan and Liu family clan of Luqiu Village in the late Qing Dyansty. In front of Zhiyuan Earthen Fortress, the rectangular Panchi (a type of ancient pool with arch bridge) is another useful facility for defense. In history, Zhiyuan Earthen Fortress was once used as a drugstore. Presently, there is only one guardian left for the fortress.

治元堡建在田中，易于防守／Zhiyuan Earthen Fortress builted in a paddy field, easy for defense

治元堡门前的长方形泮池／Rectangle deep pool in front of the gate of Zhiyuan Earthen Fortress

福安堡外景／Outdoor scene of Fu'an Earthen Fortress

堡门／Gate of the earthen fortress

## 福安堡（永安）

位于永安市青水畲族乡三房村乌坑自然村，坐北向南，占地面积1200平方米，三层，建筑面积1900平方米。该堡由乌坑钟氏建造，清朝咸丰年间，以钟成登为首的六人，为全族安危决定建堡。经过多年风雨，福安堡外观保存尚好，堡内目前仅住有一户人家。

---

## Fu'an Earthen Fortress (Yong'an)

Fu'an Earthen Fortress is located in Wukeng Unincorporated Village, Sanfang Village, Qingshui She Ethnic Group Township, Yong'an City. It is a three-storey building facing south with an area of 1200 square meters and a gross floor area of 1900 square meters. The fortress is built by Zhong family clan in Wukeng. During the rein of Emperor Xianfeng in Qing Dynasty, six people headed by Zhong Chengdeng decided to build it for the safety of the entire clan. After vicissitudes of time, the appearance of Fu'an Earthen Fortress is preserved. Now there is only one household living in the fortress.

堡内为三层楼建筑／The three-storey building in the earthen fortress

土堡内的杂货店／Grocery store in the earthen fortress

燕归来／Returning swallows

## 慎修堡（永安）

　　位于永安市小陶镇大陶口村，又称正远楼，内设慎修堂。该堡坐西南向东北，占地面积约3500平方米，建筑面积约3200平方米，为大陶口村张氏张振吉建于清朝道光十六年（1836年）。慎修堡面积大，堡内建筑层次分明，多而不乱，设计科学，采光良好。目前，土堡尚有几户人家居住，堡内墙壁留存有"文化大革命"时期的标语，成为一个时代的印记。

## Shenxiu Earthen Fortress (Yong'an)

　　Also known as Zhengyuan Building, Shenxiu Earthen Fortress is located in Dataokou Village, Xiaotao Town, Yong'an City. There is a Shenxiu Hall within it. The whole structure faces northeast with an area of about 3500 square meters and a gross floor area of about 3200 square meters. It is built by Zhang Zhengji, member of Zhang family clan in Dataokou Village in the 16th year during the rein of Emperor Daoguang in Qing Dynasty (1836 AD). In a large scale, the fortress has a proper arrangement of interior structures, which are in a large number and good order with scientific design and good natural lighting. Presently, there are only several families living inside the fortress. On the walls of the fortress, there are the slogans left during the Cultural Revolution, the symbol of an era.

慎修堡全景／The entire scenery of Shenxiu Earthen Fortress

慎修堡采光较好／Comparatively better lighting equipment of Shenxiu Earthen Fortress

时代的标语，记录一个特殊的年代／Slogans of an era, recording a special age

水井／Well

## 永峙楼（永安）

　　位于永安市小陶镇新寨村，坐西北向东南，占地面积2060平方米，土堡三层，建筑面积2230平方米。永峙楼始建于清朝道光二年（1822年），由朱氏合族所建。永峙楼目前已无人居住，堡内原有祖祠，已被拆。

## Yongzhi Earthen Fortress (Yong'an)

　　Yongzhi Earthen Fortress is located in Xinzhai Village, Xiaotao Town, Yong'an City. It is a three-storey structure facing southeast with an area of 2060 square meters and a gross floor area of 2230 square meters. Built in the 2nd year during the rein of Emperor Daoguang in Qing Dynasty by Zhu family clan, it now houses no residents. The former ancestral shrine in it has been demolished.

永峙楼外景／Outdoor scene of Yongzhi Earthen Fortress

土堡已无人居住，依旧存放着写了名字的寿材/The earthen fortress which now houses no residents, a coffin with a name in it

不同时代的标语，雨梗墙上的彩绘历久弥新／Slogans of different eras, the long-lasting colored drawings in Yugeng Walls

永盛楼全景／Entire scenery of Yongsheng Earthen Fortress

堡门／Gate of the earthen fortress

## 永盛楼（永安）

　　位于永安市小陶镇寨中村，坐北向南，土堡占地面积1200平方米，三层，建筑面积2800平方米。永盛楼建造年代大概是清朝，由当地朱氏家族所建。现土堡外观尚存，但已无人居住，土堡后人在堡外建房，堡内建筑已经不存，仅经过简单修缮。

---

## Yongsheng Earthen Fortress (Yong'an)

　　Yongsheng Earthen Fortress is located in Zhaizhong Village, Xiaotao Town, Yong'an City. It is a three-storey structure facing south with an area of 1200 square meters and a gross floor area of 2800 square meters). Built in about Qing Dynasty by the local Zhu family clan, the appearance of the fortress is well preserved. But it houses no residents now. The offspring of the fortress built houses outside it while the interior architectures are not preserved after some simple renovations.

永盛楼内建筑早已拆光，只剩空荡荡的大坪／The interior structures inside Yongsheng Building has been demolished, with an empty ground left

神位、信仰／A memorial tablet faith

## 允升堡（永安）

位于永安市八一镇八一村张坑自然村中部，土堡建在山间盆地水田间的一个小山包上，占地面积2500平方米，建筑面积2670平方米。该堡为当地朱氏朱廷扬建于清朝咸丰九年（1858年），堡名由清朝宁洋县县令题词。土堡目前无人居住，堡内建筑尚完好，当地朱氏后裔曾经集资进行初步维护。

### Yunsheng Earthen Fortress (Yong'an)

Yunsheng Earthen Fortress is located in the middle part of Zhangkeng Unincorporated Village, Bayi Village, Bayi Town, Yong'an City. Located in a paddy field beside a hilltop in a basin, it covers an area of 2500 square meters and a gross floor area of 2670 square meters. Built in the 9th year during the rein of Xianfeng in Qing Dynasty (1858 AD) by Zhu Tingyang, member of the local Zhu family clan, it was named by the magistrate of Ningyang County in Qing Dynasty. The fortress now houses no residents. The interior structures are preserved well. The offspring of the local Zhu family clan have conducted a preliminary maintenance of the fortress after fund-raising.

堡门／Gate of the earthen fortress

允升堡外景／Outdoor scene of Yunsheng Earthen Fortress

会清堡外景／Outdoor scene of Huiqing Earthen Fortress

## 会清堡（永安）

位于永安市西洋镇福庄中南部，坐北向南，土堡占地面积2300平方米，建筑面积2356平方米。会清堡由当地邢氏先祖于清朝乾隆二十年（1755年）始建，历经数年营造而成。会清堡具备土堡的各种防御元素，利用河流做天然屏障。土堡内建有多个书斋，人文气息浓厚，装饰精巧，独具匠心。土堡现已无人居住，外墙也有几处坍塌，亟待整修。

## Huiqing Earthen Fortress (Yong'an)

Huiqing Earthen Fortress is located in the middle and southern part of Fuzhuang, Xiyang Town, Yong'an City. Facing south, it covers an area of 2300 square meters and a gross floor area of 2356 square meters. Begun to be built by the ancestors of the local Xing family clan in the 20th year during the rein of Emperor Qianlong in Qing Dynasty (1755 AD), it took several years to be completed. All elements of defense combined, it makes advantage of the river to set a natural line of defense. There are many study rooms inside the fortress, creating a dense cultural atmosphere with exquisite and ingenious decorations. The fortress now houses no residents. Several walls collapsed, requiring for an entire revamp.

堡门上的石雕、檐上草青青／Gate of an earthen fortress,stones sculptures,thriving grass on the eaves

会清堡利用河流作为天然屏障／Huiqing Earthen Fortress has made rivers into a natural defense

被蔓草掩盖的时光／Impress of time covered by creeping weeds

糟朽的梁柱，难敌风雨侵蚀／Exquisite beams, failing to flight against the erosion of wind and rains

邓家土堡外景／Outdoor scene of Dengjia Earthen Fortress

农具／Agricultural implements

## 邓家土堡（清流）

　　又称上土堡，位于清流县灵地镇邓家北面的田中村，坐北朝南，土堡占地面积2700平方米，建筑面积2200平方米。邓家土堡创建人为本地人邓承御，他于清朝康熙四十三年（1704年）开始建造土堡自保。土堡外墙基本以夯土为主，南大门外，有一口池塘作为护堡壕。现土堡有多处坍塌，堡内仅一户人家居住。

## Dengjia Earthen Fortress (Qingliu)

Also known as Shangtu Earthen Fortress, it is located in Tianzhong Village to the north of Deng family clan, Lingdi Town, Qingliu County. Facing south, it covers an area of 2700 square meters and a gross floor area of 2200 square meters. The builder of Dengjia Earthen Fortress is Deng Chengyu, a native of the area. In the 43rd year during the rein of Emperor Kangxi in Qing Dynasty (1704), he began to build the fortress for self-defense. The exterior walls are made up of the rammed earth. Outside the southern gate, there is a pool set for defense. Now many parts of the fortress have collapsed. The fortress now houses only one household.

跑马道上的寿材／Coffins in the racing course

福州土堡群主要集中在永泰县、闽清县和福清市等山区。福州土堡多建在河边山冈上或台地上，依山势而建。福州土堡多称寨或庄，大多为当地某一姓氏家族所建，而且使用率较高，即使无人居住的土堡，家族成婚或祭祖的一些仪式，依然会在土堡中举行，生活化气息浓厚。

其中，永泰县的土堡主要集中在永泰、德化交界的几个乡镇，堡内土木结构建筑多，目前尚有人居住的土堡也较多。闽清县的土堡多以土木结构、中部堂屋、正立面两侧建四面坡碉式角楼的民居为主，特色明显。此外，福州也有针对倭寇进犯而建的堡垒式建筑，多以毛石块垒就，内设炮台、炮口。

Fuzhou Earthen Fortresses are mainly scattered in Yongtai County, Minqing County, Fuqing City and other mountainous regions. Mostly located on the hillock along the river or in the platforms, they are built according to the conditions of mountains. Most of Fuzhou earthen fortresses are called as Stockaded Village or Village. In many cases, the fortress was built by a particular local family clan with many of them still being used. Even in those fortresses which now house no residents, marriages or ancestor worships are still held inside them, creating a dense life-oriented atmosphere.

Many earthen fortresses are mainly located in several townships and towns on the boundary between Yongtai and Dehua. with many of which were built in civil engineering structure. Presently, many earthen fortresses still house residents. The earthen fortresses in Minqing County are mainly built in civil engineering structure, with central rooms in the center and fort-type turrets built on both sides of the façade, making its own features more distinctive. Besides, there are buildings resembling a castle for defending against the Japanese pirates, which were built by boulder strips and with structures like battery and gun muzzles.

东关寨全景／Entire scenery of Dongguan Stockaded Village

## 东关寨（福清）

　　位于福清市一都镇东山村，由当地何姓家族兴建于清朝乾隆元年（1736年）。寨堡坐西向东，依山势而建，层层递升，占地面积达4000多平方米。东关寨外部为防御性极强的堡垒结构，内部却是适合生活起居的传统福州民居结构。东关寨所处山头遍植枇杷，成熟季节，满山飘香。2011年，东关寨被列入福建省级重点文物保护单位。

## Dongguan Stockaded Village (Fuqing)

　　Dongguan Stockaded Village is located in Dongshan Village, Yidu Town, Fuqing City. It was built by the local He family clan in the 1st year during the rein of Emperor Qianlong (1736 AD) in Qing Dynasty. Facing east, it was built down the hillside in ascending stages, covering an area of above 4000 square meters. The exterior part is characteristic of a fortress with strong defending functions while the interior part is a traditional Fuzhou civil dwelling fit for living. In the hill where Dongguan Stockaded Village is located, there grows loquat, which emitted a fragrance perfuming the entire mountain when ripe. In 2011, Dongguan Stockaded Village was listed as Key Culture Relic Protection Unit of Fujian Province.

被枇杷树包围的东关寨/Dongguan Stockaded Village surrounded the loquat trees

厚实的堡墙/Strongly fortified walls

厅堂／Hall

东关寨内房屋众多，纵横相连/Numerous houses inside Dongguan Stockaded Village, linked together vertically and horizontally

天井下的风景／Scenery under a skylight

柱础上的精美石刻／Exquisite stone sculptures in column bases

坚固的堡墙／Solid walls

## 娘寨（闽清）

位于闽清县省潢镇良寨村外一座大山深处，占地面积约1000平方米。传说旧时此处张氏人家因与外姓发生纠纷，在一场械斗中几遭灭绝，唯祖母与一个小孙子幸免于难。此后，这位张姓祖母历尽千辛万苦，独力抚养小孙子长大成人，并用三年的时间建起了一座寨堡。"娘寨"就此得名。寨内目前已无人居住，但张氏后人正在集资大修。

## Niang Stockaded Village (Minqing)

Niang Stockaded Village is tucked away in a big mountain outside Niang Village, Shenghuang Town, Minqing County. It covers an area of about 1000 square meters. Stories came down to us that due to conflicts with other family clans, the residents – Zhang family clan were almost diminished during a fight with only a grandmother and her grandchild surviving it. After then, the grandmother went through innumerable hardships to foster the grandchild into an adult by her own efforts and used three years to build up a stockaded village. Thus, the village was named as "Niang Stockaded Village" (literally means mother's village). Now the village accomodates no residents. But the offspring of Zhang family clan has raised a fund to conduct a major repair.

娘寨全景／Entire scenery of Niang Stockaded Village

娘寨现已在整修中，成为当地张氏的宗祠所在／Niang Stockaded Village under repair, which is also the place of the ancestral hall of Zhang family clan in the local area

## 品亨寨（闽清）

又名岐庐，位于闽清县坂东镇溪峰村。建造人张鸣岐，为清朝进士，官至九江知府。清朝咸丰三年（1853年）动工，清朝咸丰八年（1858年）建成，占地面积6000多平方米，建筑面积4400多平方米。岐庐建成之后曾多次经历战乱烽火，均安然无恙，其内部建筑保存完好，装饰精美。

## Pingheng Stockaded Village (Minqing)

Also known as Qi Cottage, Pingheng Stockaded Village is located in Xifeng Village, Bandong Town, Minqing County. Its builder Zhang Mingqi is a successful candidate in the imperial civil examination in Qing Dynasty. He was then promoted to Magistrate of Jiujiang Prefecture. Built in the 3rd year during the rein of Emperor Xianfeng in Qing Dynasty (1853 AD), it was completed in the 8th year during the rein of Emperor Xianfeng. It covers an area of over 6000 square meters and a gross floor area of over 4400 square meters. After completion, Qi Cottage suffered scourges of wars and tumultuous times, and yet it survived. Its interior structures are preserved well with exquisite decorations.

品亨寨外景／Outdoor scene of Pingheng Stockaded Village

品亨寨结合了福州传统建筑和土堡的建筑特点／Pinheng Stockaded Village combining the architectural features of traditional architectures of Fuzhou and the earthen fortresses

天井／Well

精美的风火墙／Exquisite fire wall

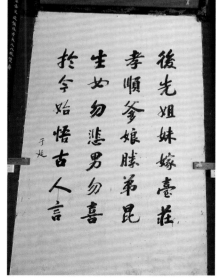

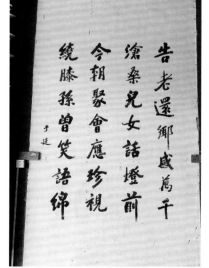

厅堂内牌匾众多／Numerous plagues in the hall

门窗装饰华丽繁复，精细费时／Complicated and resplendent windows and door decorations, once taking delicate efforts and a lot of time to be completed

门窗装饰华丽繁复，精细费时／Complicated and resplendent windows and door decorations, once taking delicate efforts and a lot of time to be completed

垂花柱上的人物木雕栩栩如生／Life-like person wood sculptures in tassel pillars

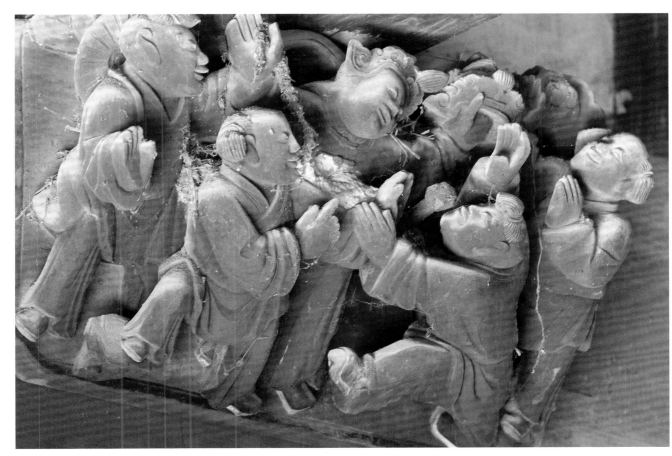

垂花柱上的人物木雕栩栩如生／Life-like person wood sculptures in tassel pillars

三新庄全景／Entire scenery of Sanxin Village

堡门／Gate of an earthen fortress

## 三新庄（闽清）

位于闽清县省璜镇三新村，土堡由当地卢氏先祖始建于清朝嘉庆年间。土堡位于路边，正面堡墙已被完全破坏，盖上了现代建筑，堡内尚有多户人家居住。

### Sanxin Village (Minqing)

Sanxin Village is located in Sanxin Village, Shenghuang Town, Minqing County. The ancestor of the local Lu family clan built it during the rein of Emperor Jiaqing in Qing Dynasty. Reposing along the road, the front walls of fortress was completely destroyed, and transformed into a modern architecture. Now the village houses several households.

堡内，生活气息浓郁／Interior structures of the fortress with a dense living atmosphere

## 绍安庄（永泰）

又名周坑寨，位于永泰县东洋乡周坑村。寨子门额题名"绍安庄"，建于清朝同治年间，占地面积4000平方米。寨子正面仅设一大门，易于防守。寨内采光通风排水好，是一座布局合理易守难攻的大宅院。周坑寨为东洋黄氏祖屋，100多年过去了，依然保持原貌，只有一些局部小改造。由于地处偏远山区，许多"文化大革命"时期的标语还保留完好，反映了一个时代的缩影。

## Shao'an Village (Yongtai)

Also known as Zhoukeng Stockaded Village, Shao'an Village is located in Zhoukeng Village, Dongyang Township, Yongtai County. The inscription above the village is the Chinese characters – "Shao'an Village". It was built during the rein of Emperor Tongzhi in Qing Dynasty, covering an area of 4000 square meters. In front of the stockaded village, there is a gate for defense. The village is rigged up with a good system of natural lighting, ventilation and drainage. The big dwelling is in proper arrangement easy for defense and hard to attack. Zhoukeng Stockaded Village is the ancestral home of Huang family clan of Dongyang. Over a century, it still retained its former appearance with little repairs in some parts. Due to its remote location in mountainous areas, many slogans in the Culture Revolution are still left, reflecting an era's epitome.

绍安庄全景／Entire scenery of Shao'an Village

绍安庄正门／Main entrance of Shao'an Village

时代的标语，岁月的缩影／Slogans of an ear, the epitome of the time

厅堂／Hall

土堡内的标语／Slogans in the Earthen Fortress

绍安庄为东洋乡黄氏祖宅，堡内建筑保存完好／Shao'an Village is the ancestral hall of Huang family clan in Dongyang Township, with interior structures being preserved

幽深的走道／Deep and far-reaching corridor

万安堡全景／Entire scenery of Wang'an Earthen Fortress

## 万安堡（永泰）

又名尾寨、太平堡，位于永泰县嵩口镇道南村北面的大樟溪畔，万安堡共三层，占地面积约3000平方米。土堡外观尚存，内部已被主人分割成条块，或建房，或出租，破坏严重。

## Wang'an Earthen Fortress (Yongtai)

Also known as Wei Stockaded Village or Taiping Earthen Fortress, Wang'an Earthen Fortress is a three-storey architecture located besides Dazhang River to the north of Daonan Villge, Songkou Town, Yongtai County. The appearance of the fortress is preserved while the interior structures has been cut or demolished to build new houses or rented, which caused severe damages.

土堡侧门／Side door of an earthen fortress

土堡人家，家有喜事／Households in the earthen fortress, happy event of a family

侧门、水槽／Side door,Trough

### 宁远庄（永泰）

位于永泰县嵩口镇月洲村，占地面积约1500平方米。据说是由永泰县第一位进士张沃的第27代孙张谦建造于清朝乾隆年间，距今已有200多年历史。寨子已无人居住，外墙部分坍塌。

### Ningyuan Village (Yongtai)

Ningyuan Village is located in Yuezhou Village, Songkou Town, Yongtai County, covering an area of about 1500 square meters. It is said to be built during the rein of Emperor Qianlong in Qing Dynasty by Zhang Qian, the 27th generation of offspring of ZhangWo, the first successful candidate in the imperial civil examination. Over 200 years later, the village now houses no people, with part of the exterior walls collapsed.

建在山坡上的宁远庄／Ningyuan Village built down the hillside

宁远庄现已无人居住，庄内供奉当地神祇张天君／Ningyuan Village now houses no residents, Zhang Tianjun, the local god consecrated in the village

宁远庄正门、堡门、张天君／Main entrance of Ningyuan Village, gate of an earthen fortress, Zhang Tianjun

## 成厚庄（永泰）

又称卢洋寨，位于永泰县嵩口镇卢洋村后山。寨前石碑资料显示，成厚庄建于明末清初，建造人陈德美始建，子孙后代几次维修，面积2000多平方米。寨子目前已无人居住，成为野狗的乐园。

### Chenghou Village (Yongtai)

Also known as Luyang Stockaded Village, Chenghou Village is located back in the mountain of Luyang Village, Songkou Town, Yongtai County, covering an area of over 2000 square meters. The old documents about the village reveals that it was built in the transitional period between Ming Dynasty and Qing Dynasty by Chen Demei. His offspring has repaired the village, which now houses no residents and turns into a wild area.

远眺成厚庄／Glancing at Chenghou Village from far

成厚庄堡墙由毛石垒就，墙体也有部分坍塌／Walls of Chenghou Village built by rubbles, with part of it collapsed

双重堡门／Gate of two layers of the earthen fortress

成厚庄内人去楼空，置身其中，给人一种凄清荒凉的感觉/Chenghou Village now houses no residents. When one comes into it, a sense of loneliness and desolation will creep into him

信仰／Faith

跑马道／Racing course

厚实的堡墙／Strongly fortified walls

## 新洋尾寨（永泰）

　　位于永泰县大洋乡大展村，寨子建于清朝嘉庆二十三年（1818年），占地面积约6000平方米。村子有两座土堡，新寨仅比旧寨晚建30年，但目前都处于被废弃的境地。新寨外墙外观保存尚完整，寨内建筑则损毁较多，唯有一颗桂花树暗暗吐芳。

## Xinyangwei Stockaded Village (Yongtai)

　　Xinyangwei Stockaded Village is located in Dazhan Village, Dayang Township, Yongtai County. Built in the 23rd year during the rein of Emperor Jiaqing in Qing Dynasty (1818 AD), it covers an area of about 6000 square meters. There are two earthen fortresses inside the village, the new one built 30 years after the completion of the old one, but both have fallen into disuse. The walls and appearance of the new fortress are preserved, but many interior structures are damaged. There is only an osmanthus tree bursting into blossom in quiet.

洋尾寨正门、美人靠／Main entrance of Yangwei Stockaded Village, Back-rest chair for beauties

宅子荒废，当年喜事的对联犹在，讲述过去的热闹／Though in waste, the couplet memorizing the happy event of the past years is still pasted there, telling us its noisy passing time

庭院内荒草杂树高过人头／Weeds and unknown trees taller than a person in the courtyard

苔藓不仅走进过道，还爬上农具/Mosses creep into the passageway and climb up to the agricultural implements

## 黄土寨（永泰）

又称紫来庄，位于永泰县大洋镇康乐村。建于清朝乾隆年间，占地面积约2000平方米。黄土寨虽然规模较小，而且正面寨墙有部分坍塌，但其内部保存却比较完善。寨子由当地汪氏先祖所建，黄土寨人才辈出，寨内"文魁"牌匾多幅。

## Huangtu Stockaded Village (Yongtai)

Huangtu Stockaded Village, also known as Zilai Village, is located in Kangle Village, Dayang Town, Yongtai County. Built during the rein of Emperor Qianlong in Qing Dynasty, it covers an area of about 2000 square meters. Also in a relatively smaller size, parts of the walls in the front of the fortress crumpled down, though the interior structures were kept rather well. The ancestors of the local Wang family clan built this fortress, which gave birth to generations of talents. Now there are several plagues written by the top men of letters left in the village.

黄土寨外景／Outdoor scene of Huangtu Stockaded Village

多块清朝"文魁"牌匾，证明这个家族出过人才／Plagues for rewarding "talented letter man" of Qing Dynasty, proving that there had been talents in this family

阳光照进无人院落／Sunlight shines into a desolate courtyard

堡门／Gate of the earthen fortress

## 康乐庄（永泰）

　　位于永泰县大洋镇康乐村。当地乡绅汪攸交建于清朝嘉庆年间，故又名攸交寨。占地面积约2000平方米。康乐庄内部建筑尚好，也有人居住，但寨墙已被汪氏后人搭建新宅，外观破坏严重。

## Kangle Village (Yongtai)

Kangle Village is located in Kangle Village, Dayang Town, Yongtai County, covering an area of about 2000 square meters. The local squire named Wang Youjiao built it during the rein of Emperor Jiaqing in Qing Dynasty, thus it was also known as Youjiao Stockaded Village. The interior structures of Kangle Village are preserved well, and it also houses some families. A new addition was built on the basis of walls, whose exterior appearance is severely damaged.

厅堂整洁，对联墨迹犹新／The village has couplets with seemingly still new characters, and a clean and tidy hall

青石堡墙／Walls of Green Stone Earthen Fortress

## 青石寨（永泰）

　　位于永泰县同安镇三捷村，因寨墙以青石垒砌而成，故得名。始建于明末，重建于清朝道光十年（1830年），耗时八年乃成，修建人张行风。寨内有楹联"龙门玉带水，鸡寨锦屏山"描述的就是青石寨风光。青石寨占地面积6000多平方米，四角均建有碉式角楼。青石寨，2011年被列为福建省级重点文物保护单位。

## Qingshi Stockaded Village (Yongtai)

　　Qingshi Stockaded Village is located in Sanjie Village, Tongan Town, Yongtai County. It was named so for the walls were made by bluestones (Qingshi in Chinese means green stones). The stockaded village was first built at the end of Ming Dynasty and restored by Zhang Xingfeng in the 10th year during the rein of Emperor Daoguang in Qing Dynasty (1830 AD). The whole project takes 8 years to be completed. There is a couplet hanging inside the fortress that reads ""In Longmen runs a stream like a jade belt, Besides Ji Village reposes Jinping Mountain, which describes the landscape of Qingshi Stockaded Village. The village covers an area of above 6000 square meters, in the four corners of which fort-type turrets were built. In 2011, it was listed as Key Cultural Relic Protection Unit of Fujian Province.

青石寨全景／The entire scene of Green Stone Stockaded Village

青石寨正厅／Main hall of Green Stone Stockaded Village

阳光照进无人院落／Sunlight shines into a desolate courtyard

无人后院，长满野草／The courtyard which houses no one, overgrown with riot weeds

厅堂、石碓／Hall, a treadle-operated tilt hammer for hulling rice

封火墙上等舌瓦，是"古代"的瓷砖／High-quality lip-like tile in a fire wall, an "ancient" tile

彩绘、柱础／Colored drawings, column base

堡墙／Walls of an earthen fortress

## 爱荆庄（永泰）

又称米石寨，位于永泰县同安镇洋尾村，建于清朝道光十二年(1832年)，建造人鲍美祚，故名"美祚寨"。至于"米石寨"之名，乃是"美祚寨"用永泰当地方言说来，与"米石寨"谐音，以讹传讹。寨子门额题名"爱荆庄"，取三田分荆之意，表示建造者希望子孙兄弟友爱之意。爱荆庄依山而建，占地面积5200平方米，气势恢宏。

### Aijing Village (Yongtai)

Aijing Village, also known as Mishi Stockaded Village, is located in Yangwei Village, Tongan Town, Yongtai County. Built by Bao Meizuo in the 12th year during the rein of Emperor Daoguang in Qing Dynasty, it was named as Mishi Stockaded Village, which is pronounced as Meizuo Stockaded Village in the local dialect of Yongtai. The Chinese characters of "Aijing Village" were carved in the plague above the gate of the village, which in Chinese means burying the hatchet with brothers, relatives or family members. It reflects that it is the builder's hope that his offspring can keep good relationships among each other, Aijing Village is a majestic architecture built alongside a hill, covering an area of 5200 square meters.

爱荆庄全景／Entire scenery of Aijing Village

三层的碉式角楼，气势恢宏/The three-storey fort-type turret, with an imposing atmosphere

厅堂/Hall

嘉禄庄外景／Outdoor scene of Jialu Village

嘉禄庄正门／Main entrance of Jialu Village

### 嘉禄庄（永泰）

又名同安寨，位于永泰县同安镇同安村。清朝咸丰二年(1852年)，乡绅张昭干、张昭容兄弟俩筹资建造，占地面积4000多平方米。当下，嘉禄庄正在大修，寨前有一湾碧水，寨内大兴土木，修葺一新。

### Jialu Village (Yongtai)

Also known as Tongan Stockaded Village, Jialu Village is located in Tong'an Village, Tong'an Town, Yongtai County. In the 2nd year during the rein of Emperor Xianfeng in Qing Dynasty (1852 AD), the squires Zhang Zhaogan and Zhang Zhaorong raised funds to build it, which now covers an area of over 4000 square meters. Presently, Jialu Stockaded Village is under a major revamp. A stretch of crystal-clear water runs in front of the village, which is on construction and exhibits a completely new look.

清河堂为宗族郡望、厅堂悬挂清光绪三年的"孝友"牌匾／Qinghe Hall belongs to a respectable and large family clan. The ancient relic hanging in the hall is a plague in honor of filial piety and brotherhood dated back to the third year under the rein of Emperor Guangxu in Qing Dynasty

寨内正在大修／The interior structures of the stockaded village is under a large-scale repair

小门一关，就是一个独立的宅院／When the door is closed, it is an unattached courtyard

生活的细节／Details of life

修竹堡全景／Entire scenery of Xiuzhu Earthen Fortress

堡门／Gate of an earthen fortress

## 修竹堡（永泰）

　　又名北山寨，位于永泰县白云乡，因为四周都是茂密的竹林，因此寨堡很难被发现，得名"修竹堡"。土堡坐南朝北，占地面积接近4000平方米，由当地何氏先祖何大瑞始建于清朝道光八年（1828年），目前土堡已无人居住，堡内建筑保存完好，木雕精美。

## Xiuzhu Earthen Fortress (Yongtai)

Also known as Beishan Stockaded Village, it is located in Baiyun Village, Yongtai County. As it is situated in a thick bamboo forest, it is difficult for others to find the village. Thus it was named as "Xiuzhu Earthen Fortress", literally means Bamboo-growing Earthen Fortress. Facing north, the fortress covers an area of almost 4000 square meters. In the 8th year during the rein of Emperor Daoguang in Qing Dynasty (1828 AD), the ancestor of the local He family clan He Darui built the fortress, which now houses no residents. The inner structures are preserved well. The wood sculptures are exquisite.

锈迹斑斑的铁门，荒草丛中的院落，诉说岁月的无情/Rusted iron walls, courtyard covered with verdure, telling us the cruelness of the time

时代的标语/Slogans of the time

堡内杂草丛生／Courtyard covered with verdure

荒草庭院／A courtyard overgrown with weeds

农具犹存，主人不在／Agricultural implements still preserved while its owner has left

## 中埔寨（永泰）

又名八卦寨，位于永泰县长庆镇中埔村，建于清朝嘉庆年间，占地面积1100多平方米。因其寨墙外观呈八角形，状如八卦，故又名八卦寨。寨堡坐北朝南，依山势而筑，寨墙下部由青石干砌而成，寨堡的主座府第为武举林孟美所建，寨墙则是其儿辈所筑，故林氏族人中便流传有"老子盖房，儿子围墙"的说法。中埔寨目前还有多户人家居住，人气颇旺，这在土堡中相当罕见。

## Zhongpu Stockaded Village (Yongtai)

Zhongpu Stockaded Village, also known as Bagua Stockaded Village, is located in Zhongpu Village, Changqing Town, Yongtai County. Built during the rein of Emperor Jiaqing in Qing Dynasty, it covers an area of over 1100 square meters. As its exterior appearance is an octagon, like the Eight Diagrams (eight combinations of three whole or broken lines formerly used in divination), it was also named as Eight Diagrams Stockaded Village. Facing south, it was built down a hillside. The underpart of the stockaded village is made up of bluestones. Lin Mengmei, the successful candidate in the imperial provincial examination built the main part of the village while his offspring walled it. It is just as the saying goes, "Father building the village while the son walling it". There are many families living inside Zhongpu Stockaded Village, creating a lively scene, which is very rare among the earthen fortresses.

中埔寨全景／Entire scenery of Zhongpu Stockaded Village

晾晒的笋干，整齐的柴火垛，中埔寨人气颇旺／Dried bamboo shoots, firewood arranged in order - Zhongpu Stockaded Village is rather vigorous

"大夫第"牌匾显示主人辉煌的过去／Glorious past revealed by the plague of Shidafu (a literati and officialdom in feudal China)

喜气洋洋的厅堂／The hall full of happiness

生机勃勃的厨房／A kitchen full of vitality

堆放在寨子里的杂物／All the sundries piled in the stockaded vilalge

过道/Passageway

精美的木雕／Exquisite wood sculptures

福建土堡的分布主要集中在三明和福州两地，除此之外，在漳州、泉州和龙岩等地也有少量分布。

漳州地区的土堡主要集中于漳浦县，有大中型城堡、小型城堡、土堡以及含有土堡建筑特点的土楼等几种类型。据不完全统计，漳浦县现存大小城堡、土堡、土楼近百座。漳州地区的土堡产生的原因有多种，一为针对倭寇进犯而建，二为防止民间械斗，维系生存需要而建。漳州土堡以三合土、块石结构居多，大型城堡中又常常建有单独的土堡。

泉州地区土堡群主要分布在德化、永春、安溪等三个山区县，这三县与三明交界，历史上互有归属，土堡这一建筑形式的出现就不足为奇。泉州土堡受三明土堡影响较大，德化土堡数量较多，但保存完好的较少，土堡内的商铺式屋宅，土堡的装饰风格，均有闽南特色。安溪的土堡主要集中在内安溪，当地人称土楼，形制外观受大田土堡影响较深。永春土堡侧重生活化，堡墙内的建筑闽南古厝风格明显，显示出宜居的特点。此外，在南安、泉港等地也有土堡元素的建筑存在，如泉港的黄素石楼、南安的土楼等等，尚有待专家考证。

龙岩地区土堡主要分布在漳平市，而且主要分布在与大田县交界的几个乡镇，其风格也受三明土堡影响较深，同时也富含客家建筑的特点。

The earthen fortresses in Fujian are mainly located in Sanming and Fuzhou. Besides, there are a few earthen fortresses situated in Zhangzhou, Quanzhou, Longyan and relevant regions.

The earthen fortresses in Zhangzhou are mainly located in Zhangpu County, which include large and middle sized castles, small-sized earthen castles, earthen fortresses and earthen structures with the architectural features of earthen fortresses. According to incomplete statistics, there are nearly one hundred large and middle sized castles, earthen fortresses and earthen structures. There are several reasons for the emergence of earthen fortresses in Zhangzhou. Firstly, it was built to defend against the Japanese pirates. Secondly, it was to prevent armed confrontation and to survive. Zhangzhou earthen fortresses were mostly built by concrete, clay and sand, in addition to block stones. In a large castle, there is often a distinct earthen fortress.

Quanhou Earthen Fortresses are mainly scattered in three mountainous counties - Dahua, Yongchun and Aixi. These three counties borders on Sanming. In history, the boundaries between the three regions and Sanming City moved several times, which made it no wonder the emergence of the earthen fortress in this region. Sanming Earthen Fortresses have a relatively greater influence on Quznhou Earthen Fortresses, many of which are located in Dehua but few are preserved well. Stores inside the fortress and the decoration style of the earthen fortresses bear the features of architectures in southern Fujian. In Anxi, the earthen fortresses are mainly located in the inner county. Many native people call it earthen structure, whose appearance is influenced by Datian Earthen Fortress. Yongchun Earthen Fortress is mainly built for residential purpose, the architectures inside which are obviously constructed in the ancient style of southern Fujian architectures and thus suitable for living. Besides, in Nanan, Quangang and relevant areas, there are also the architectures bearing the features of earthen fortress, such as Huangsushi Mansion in Quangang, earthen structures in Nanan, and etc., which await investigation of experts.

Longyan Earthen Fortresses are mostly located in Zhangping City- several counties and towns which borders on Datian County, whose style has been influenced by Sanming Earthen Fortresses and bearing the features of Hakka architectures.

泰安堡全景／Entire scenery of Tai'an Earthen Fortress

## 泰安堡（漳平）

　　位于漳平市灵地乡易坪村。该堡始建于清朝乾隆三十三年（1768年），于清朝乾隆四十五年（1780年）建成，工程历时十三年。创建者许国榜，易坪村许姓十二世祖。泰安堡坐北朝南，占地面积2000平方来，建筑面积1700平方米，是一座围廊式土木结构的厅堂院落式城堡建筑。泰安堡内已无住户，2005年被列入第六批省级文物保护单位名录。

## Tai'an Earthen Fortress (Zhangping)

　　Tai'an Earthen Fortress is located in Yiping Village, Lingdi Township, Zhangping City. Launched in the 33rd year during the rein of Emperor Qianlong in Qing Dynasty, the project was completed in the 45th year during the rein of Emperor Qianlong in Qing Dynasty (1780 AD), taking a 13-year effort. The builder Xu Guobang is the 12th generation ancestor of Xu family clan in Yiping Village. Facing south, it covers an area of 2000 square meters and a gross floor area of 1700 square meters. It is the architecture in civil engineering structure, resembling a castle, containing halls and courtyards with galleries. Now Tai'an Earthen Fortress houses no residents. In 2005, Xunlai Village was listed as 6th Batch of Key Culture Relic Protection Unit of Fujian Province.

层层叠叠的堡内建筑／Overlapping structures inside the fortress

土堡正门／Main entrance of the earthen fortress

堡内设计极为精巧／Rather exquisite designs inside the earthen fortress

层层叠叠的堡内建筑／Overlapping structures inside the fortress

许氏先祖墓碑／Tomb Stones of the ancestors of Xu family clan of the Earthen Fortress

泰安堡经过修缮，对外开放／Tai'an Earthen Fortress now opened to the public after renovation

赵家堡外景／Outdoor scene of Zhaojia Earthen Fortress

堡门／Gate of an earthen fortress

## 赵家堡（漳浦）

　　位于漳浦县湖西乡硕高山，是赵宋皇族后裔于明朝万历二十八年（1600年）建造，并世代聚居的城堡。全堡占地115390平方米，平面基本呈方形，城墙以条石砌筑，厚2.5米，高3米至4米，墙上三合土城垛高约1.5米，筑四个城门，城门上建城楼。内城中心有楼，称"完璧楼"，取"完璧归赵"之意，楼为三合土夯筑。赵家堡具备了城池的军事防御功能，完璧楼则体现了同期闽南地区民居防寇的建筑特色，城堡仿效了开封城的规划布局。

## Zhaojia Earthen Fortress (Zhangpu)

　　Zhaojia Earthen Fortress is located in Shuogao Mountain, Huxi Township, Zhangpu County. It was built by the offspring of the Emperor Zhao Kuangyi in Song Dynasty in the 28th year during the rein of Emperor Wanli in Ming Dynasty (1600 AD). It is a castle where several generations of the posterity of Emperor Zhao Kuangyi lived. It covers an area of 11.5391 hectares, with a square floor plan. The walls are built by boulder strips, each of which is 2.5 meters in thinckness and 3 to 4 meters in length. The battlement on the walls is about 1.5 in height. Gate towers are built over four gates. Inside the fortress, there is a building called "Wanbi Building", which means returning a thing intact to its owner in Chinese. The whole architecture is built in lime, clay and sand. Zhaojia Earthen Fortress functions as a fortress with military functions, inside which Wanbi Building embodies the building features of civil buildings of southern Fujian of the same period. The entire fortress imitated the layout of Kaifeng City.

外城墙内，有五座五进府第，最高建筑为完璧楼／Inside the walls of outer city, there is a mansion consisted of five arrays of rooms with the highest building named as Wanbi Building

堡内建筑，岁月爬上墙头／The interior structures of the earthen fortress; the walls were eroded in the time

完璧楼是赵家堡的核心建筑，高20米，共三层，保存完好/Wangbi Building is the core building of Zhaojia Earthen Fortress. Standing 20 meters high, there are three storey in it, all preserved well

精美的石雕，依稀可见皇家气度／Exquisite stone sculptures, the touch of the royal style can still be seen

堡内，生活气息浓郁／Interior structures of the fortress with a dense living atmosphere

城堡生活，日出而作，日落而息／Life in the earthen fortress, rising up at the break of the day and resting at the sunset

古树、古碑、历史在这里停步／Ancient tree, plague of antiquity, the step of history stopping here

古碑／Plagues of antiquity

精美的石雕／Exquisite stone sculptures

精美的石鼓／An exquisite drum-shaped stone blocks

堡门/Gate of an earthen fortress

## 诒安堡（漳浦）

位于漳浦县湖西乡，距离赵家堡约三千米路程，为赵家堡的姊妹堡，是一座保存基本完好、具有历史价值的民间军事城堡。诒安堡始建于清朝康熙二十六年（1687年），为清正一品官员黄性震所建。黄曾献"平台十策"，为收复台湾立下大功，诒安堡得名就是因其生平的"一言安台"。诒安堡城墙巍峨壮丽，气势非凡，城墙周长1200米，用巨大条石筑就。堡内街道整齐有序，95座房屋历经几百年风雨，保存尚好。

---

### Yi'an Earthen Fortress (Zhangpu)

Yi'an Earthen Fortress is located in Huxi Township, Zhangpu County. About three kilometers away from Zhaojia Earthen Fortress, it is a twin fortress of Zhaojia Earthen Fortress. As a basically well preserved fortress, it has military functions with historic value. It was built in the 26th year during the rein of Emperor Kangxi in Qing Dynasty (1687 AD) by Huang Xingzhen, the first-rank officer in Qing Dynasty. Huang Xingzhen put forward "Ten Policies on Conquering Taiwan", which made a vital contribution to the resuming of Taiwan. Yi'an Earthen Fortress was named for his achievements – "Yiyan Antai", which means Conquering Taiwan by Words in Chinese. Built by giant boulder strips, the walls of Yi'an Earthen Fortress are towering and magnificent, creating a majestic atmosphere. The perimeter of the walls is 1200 meters. Inside the fortress, the streets are arranged in order. After vicissitudes of time, 95 buildings are still preserved well.

诒安堡城墙全用巨大条石筑就，气势非凡/Built by gigantic strip stones, the walls of Yi'an Earthen Fortress is extraordinarily magnificent

经数百年风雨侵蚀，城堡保存完好/After the erosion of a century's wind and rains, the castle is still preserved well

诒安堡外景／Outdoor scene of Yi'an Earthen Fortress

城堡内规划合理，街道均为条石铺就／The castle has a proper layout, with streets paved with strip stones

石头是城堡最重要的建筑语言／Stones are the most important architectural languages of a castle

民俗活动、宗教信仰在这里都可找到／Activities of folk-customs and religious faith can be found here

## 天宝寨（芗城）

　　位于芗城区天宝镇大寨村，城堡始建于明朝万历三十一年（1603年），寨平面呈圆形，原系夯土墙楼寨，清朝乾隆二年（1737年）当地武举韩彬带头重修，改为砖墙。寨占地面积约40000平方米，环寨共有108开间，二层，各户有自用楼梯，条石基，砖墙。环楼中有平房百余间。寨辟三门，南门为正门，门上方嵌清朝乾隆二年重修时所刻"天宝寨"匾，南门内有显应庙。

堡门/Gate of an earthen fortress

## Tianbao Stockaded Village (Xiangcheng)

　　Located in Dazhai Village, Tianbao Town, Xiangcheng District, Tianbao Stockaded Village was built in the 31st year during the rein of Emperor Wangli in Qing Dynasty. The village was a round architecture surrounded by walls made up of rammed earth. In the 2nd year during the rein of Emperor Qianlong(1737), Han Bin, a successful military candidate in the imperial provincial exam took the lead in rebuilding it and transforming the earth walls into brick walls. The village now covers an area of 40000 square meters, consisting of 108 standard rooms on two floors encircling the center of the village and a building made up of about a hundred rooms. Every household within the village has their own staircase, foundations of block stones and brick walls. There are three gates in the village, with the southern gate being the main entrance. Above the southern gate, there hangs a horizontal inscribed board with the characters of "Tianbao Stockaded Village", which was made in the 2nd year during the rein of Emperor Qianlong. Inside the southern gate, there is a Xianying Temple.

天宝寨全景/The entire scene of Tianbao Stockaded Village

天宝寨就是一个古代的社区，宗祠、庙宇、民居都在里面／Tianbao Stockaded Village is an ancient community, consisting of an ancestral hall, a temple, and civil dwellings

巽来庄全景/The entire scene of Xunlai Village

## 巽来庄（永春）

又名山美土楼，位于永春县五里街的仰贤村。为清朝盐官林悠凤于乾隆四十二年(1777年)所建，占地3100平方米。巽来庄坐北朝南，一共有东、西、南三个楼门。整座楼的平面呈现出繁体的"囬（回）"字形。庄内为闽南典型的民居建筑，和古厝相似。巽来庄，2005年被列为第六批福建省级文物保护单位。

## Xunlai Village (Yongchun)

Xunlai Village, also known as Shanmei Earthen Structure, is located in Yangxian Village, Wuli Street, Yongchun County. It was built by Lin Youfeng, the salt administration officer in Qing Dynasty in the 42th year during the rein of Emperor Qianlong in Qing Dynasty (1777 AD), covering an area of 3100 square meters. Facing south, there are three gates in the eastern, western and southern directions. The floor plan of the entire building resembles the traditional Chinese character of "Hui". In 2005, Xunlai Village was listed as 6th Batch of Key Culture Relic Protection Unit of Fujian Province.

庄内的红地砖，显示出庄子的闽南色彩／Red tiles in the village, reflecting the features of southern Fujian

土堡人家，市井烟火/Households in the earthen fortress, life of ordinary people

厚重的堡墙／Strongly fortified gate

## 大兴堡 （德化）

　　位于德化县三班镇三班村。大兴堡外观尚存，土堡由当地郑氏先祖郑晟始建于清朝康熙六十一年(1722年)。土堡内院中心南北并列两幢一字形楼房，两楼之间形成东西向的干道。有专家考证，这种建筑格局是两排商铺式屋宅，中间有宽敞的中轴街巷，是典型的贸易场所。土堡也许曾经是陶瓷交易的集散地。

---

## Daxing Earthen Fortress (Dehua)

　　Daxing Earthen Fortress is located in Sanban Village, Sanban Town, Dehua County. The appearance of the earthen fortress was still preserved. It was built by Zheng Sheng – the ancestor of the local Zheng family clan – in the 61st year during the rein of Emperor Kangxi in Qing Dynasty (1722 AD). In the center of the court yard of the earthen fortress, there are two buildings resembling the Chinese number "one", between which the artery runs across it. Some experts found after textual research that this architectural structure consists of two arrays of stores, between which are wide streets and alleys on the central axis, thus playing the function of a typical place of trade. The earthen fortress was once the distribution center of ceramics.

堡门／Gate of an earthen fortress

大兴堡全景／The entire scene of Daxing Earthen Fortress

有专家考证，堡内宽阔的走道证明这里曾是陶瓷交易中心／According to the textual research of experts, the wide passageway proves that it was once the trade center of ceramics

厚德堡全景／The entire scene of Houde Earthen Fortress

厚德堡正门／Main entrance of Houde Earthen Fortress

## 厚德堡（德化）

又称祥光土楼，位于德化县水口镇祥光村。该堡由当地江氏先祖江开安始建，土堡落成于清朝道光十七年（1837年）。此堡位于大山深处，从水口镇镇区进去，尚需经过九曲十八弯，一个多小时的山路。厚德堡靠山而建，属于坡地形土堡，土堡外形壮观，两边两个角楼，加上红墙的外观，颇有几分紫禁城午门的风采。

---

## Houde Earthen Fortress (Dehua)

Houde Earthen Fortress, also known as Xiangguang Earthen Structure, is located in Xiangguang Village, Shuikou Town, Dehua County. It was built by Jiang Kaian, the local Jiang family clan in the 17th year during the rein of Emperor Daoguang in Qing Dynasty (1837 AD). Tucked away among mountains, it takes over an hour's effort to approach it, starting from Shuikou Town and then trudging through many twists and turns. Built down the hillside, it has a magnificent appearance, in the structure belonging to the earthen fortress on the slopes. There are two turrets in the fortress, whose walls are red, resembling the style of the Forbidden City to some degree.

楼阁式角楼，精巧别致／Building-type turret, exquisite and unconventional

庭院草青青／Flourishing weeds in the courtyard

灰尘满厅堂／Hall covered with dirt

传统农具／Agricultural implements